Reviews

I really love it. In fact, I told my husband that he needs to read it. It's just a great "read" and it's hard to put down, even on the second or third read. It has a fast pace, which is a good sign, and you have to keep reading to see what happens next. All in all, it's perfect.

— SHIRLEY HOLGATE, RETIRED CALPOLY STATE UNIVERSITY 30-YEAR ENGLISH PROFESSOR.

Some books make us laugh. Some make us cry. Others teach us or amuse us for a short while. But most books are soon forgotten. "I Became a Vagabond Traveler, living a roaming, carefree existence" will make you laugh and cry. It will teach and amuse you. It is not a story that you will forget. The courage of this young girl will make you want to wind back the clock, be twenty-two again, and explore the whole wide world. The adventures in Aline's memoirs are the stories that great movies are made of.

— BECKY WHITE, AUTHOR OF DOUBLE LUCK, MEMOIRS OF A CHINESE ORPHAN; AND BETSY ROSS, HOLIDAY HOUSE.

— RETIRED EXECUTIVE EDITOR OF SHINING STAR AND A NEW DAY MAGAZINES.

Aline, a continental vagabond, deserves a Masters degree for her vivid descriptions of people and places in Europe, New York, Oregon, The Republic of Panama, and the South Seas. She relates with clarity and alacrity, stunning stories of European adventures and tantalizing tales of the South Pacific. At times, she seems to find a measure of joy amid grossly deficient living conditions and lack of personal effects. The author keeps readers captivated and anxious to continue from each page to the next. You will find this a delightful read.

— ALANA M. H. RETIRED CLINICAL LABORATORY SUPERVISOR, AND SCIENTIST.

I stayed up late, reading the whole book in one night. It is an inspiring story, a lovely example of a young woman's determination to rise above her dysfunctional childhood - to see the world, learn how others live, and make a happy life for herself and her own family. The book left me wanting to know more.

— JUDY G, RETIRED FAMILY THERAPIST

I Became a Vagabond Traveler, living a roaming carefree existence, was an excellent read. I was very impressed by Aline's courage and fortitude in seeing what could be experienced if one risks the normal comforts. Aline explored life as it came and created a stronger sense of herself to develop a deeper self identity. I believe this book shows the heroism of an individual who has the courage to explore the unknown and really gain insight into what is possible. After reading Aline's book, I am prompted to travel. The book flowed smoothly and I couldn't wait for the next experience.

— PHIL W, RETIRED MENTAL HEALTH SUPERVISOR

So many places, an outstanding life! Aline lived and experienced more than one could have learned from any text book. It was hard to put the book down.

— COLLEEN D. RETIRED RETAIL SALES

A fascinating read. It carries one over the waves of many continents and oceans. It is a book that must be read! I couldn't put the book down!

— ELIZABETH, MASTER'S DEGREE IN FAMILY SYSTEMS FROM THE UNIVERSITY OF ST. THOMAS, AND EXTENSIVE STUDIES AT THE CARL JUNG CENTER, IN HOUSTON, TX

ISBN: 1482650754

ISBN 13: 9781482650754

Library of Congress Control Number: 2013903997

CreateSpace Independent Publishing Platform

North Charleston, South Carolina

To Dave & Gail

I Became A
Vagabond Traveler

living a roaming carefree existence.

Eileen Carpenter

By

AKA *Madame Aline*

Acknowledgements

My deepest gratitude to my dear friend Shirley H., who willingly and patiently edited my memoirs; and to Becky White, who tirelessly edited my book, twice, and threw so many ideas at me and kept me on the right track; and to Daniela Kanz, who helped me through the many computer challenges; and to so many friends and acquaintances who urged me throughout the years to write down my stories.

I dedicate this book to:

my son, Robert Arthur
my daughter, Karina Eileen
my granddaughter, Lorraine (Lori) Aline

My Goal Was To Find Becky White

About ten years ago I was given a book about Lu Chi Fa, a Chinese orphan. The book, "Double Luck," was written by Becky White. Somehow I found out that Lu Chi Fa was born and lived in the same town in China as a dear friend of mine. I first met Jooleng while I was renting a room in Singapore from her daughter. We remained lifelong friends. Then several years ago I gave a copy of the book to Jooleng while I was visiting her in Vancouver, Canada. She sat on her rocker for two days with the book in hand. She read a little, then dozed a little, then read a little, always with the book on her lap. Her daughter said it was the best thing I could have given her.

I always had Becky White in the back of my mind, and the fact that I had to find her when my memoirs were approaching finalization. Then just a couple of years ago while at a church women's luncheon I noticed the book "Double Luck" on a bookshelf. I instantly realized I was in Becky's home. Now that was double luck.

Since then we have become close friends and she has helped me so much in my goal to publish my memoirs.

So many, many thanks Becky.

Contents

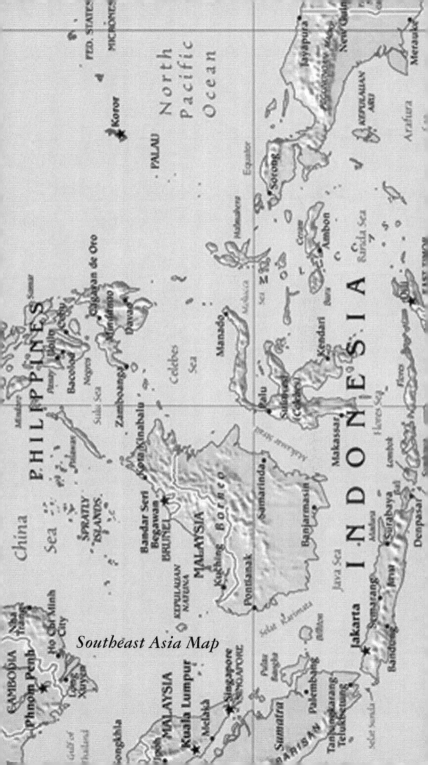

Southeast Asia Map

Prologue

I have often been asked why I left Canada and never returned other than to visit. Since this was my life, I guess I never knew any differently, although now I envy those who kept close family ties, went on to college, married young, raised a healthy and happy family, and then stayed married for the next 40, 50, 60 years and more.

Well, that was not my life. I lost my brother to Leukemia when he was eighteen and I was seventeen. After that, my adoptive mother would often look at his picture as he lay in his coffin and tell me that it should have been me. It was well known in the family that I had been adopted as a playmate for my brother and for the next seventeen years suffered the abuses from both him and my mother. After his death, she took in four male university students, and I continued my Cinderella role in the family.

One thing I have always been thankful for is my determination. I guess it is hidden away in my genes to move forward; with that in mind, I ran away from home when I was eighteen. I went to live with an uncle and his wife, a favorite brother of my mother's, to whom she never spoke again.

For the next few years, I worked at double jobs until I had enough saved to leave Canada and travel to Europe. I never did go back to live in my home city, or even country, as it always made me nervous to even think about being in proximity to my mother. For several years during visits home, I would faithfully visit her but again it made me extremely nervous. Eventually I dropped out of her life for the next 22 years.

I remember once when my two children were three and four years old, we were visiting an aunt and old grandma; the talk centered around this person's mother and that person's mother to which I had nothing to add. That evening while lying in bed, my young son whispered, "Mom, how come Aunt Dale has a mother, and Aunt Sal has a mother, and Karina and I have a mother. Where is your mother? I froze as I had long dreaded and mused over my response to such a question. Before my mind could conjure a response, my young son said, "It's okay Mom; if I ever ask that question again, just hold your hand up and say 'STOP!' and I'll understand." True to his word, he never again brought up the subject. The words, "your mother" did come up in family conversations from time to time, and several years later my young daughter questioned this. I was able to satisfy her curiosity by simply saying, "Oh that was someone that Grandpa was married to at one time." My children never knew the existence of my mother until they were in their early twenties. After 30 years of estrangement, my parents remarried and the horrors began again.

It was my dear paternal Grandmother who insisted that I remain in the family when the adoption agency came to her farm to take me back when I was barely one-year old. Due to my mother's infidelities, I often lived for periods of time with my numerous aunts and uncles on both sides of the family. It is thanks to each and every one of them that I survived those years. They are all still very close and dear to my heart, and I will always be grateful to them.

It still bothers me that I never had my very own mother; someone to talk to and to be close to, someone who would love me unconditionally.

Before departing Canada in 1960

Sailing From Vancouver

That was so many tender, mystical years ago. They were years of my youth when a young 22-year-old girl was reaching out for life trying to find my niche in this world and searching wherever my adventurous spirit would take me. There had to be something just waiting to touch my life. It was so many years ago, but memories are powerful feelings and they flow back into my heart as if it were yesterday.

I left my home in Vancouver, Canada, in June 1960, on one of the P. & O. Line's luxury cruise ships, the Orsova. My girl friend, Lillian, and I sailed down the coast of Washington, Oregon, California, Central America, through the Panama Canal, the Caribbean and the Atlantic. Three weeks later, we arrived in La Havre, France, and crossed the English Channel landing at Dover, England. From there we took a train to London.

I had worked two jobs the four years prior, brown bagging my lunches and saving every single penny in order to buy a car. Of course, at that time I did not have the dream of traveling, but it enfolded as soon as Lillian and I made the decision to take off for Europe. The plan was to visit my former Scottish room-mate, Kathleen, who had recently returned to her home in Aberdeen, Scotland. Beyond that we had no idea of how long we would stay or what the future would hold.

The highlight of our trip aboard the Orsova from Vancouver to London was the crossing of the Panama Canal. We were not allowed to disembark at Panama City as all ships were on a tight time schedule in the queue to get through the locks. Several large buffets were set out just inside the railings of the ship where we indulged our gastronomic appetites. The excitement level was high.

The Canal was 32 years in the making and was completed in 1914. The locks are 300' wide and split North America and South America in an inter-oceanic crossing between the Pacific and Atlantic Oceans, accommodating both pleasure and business crafts. We learned that the water level on the Pacific side is 19 feet higher than the Atlantic side. As we entered the canal from the Pacific side, the ship was raised 52 feet through the Miraflores Locks. A few miles later, the ship was raised another 30 feet at the Pedro Miguel Locks. Then we cruised 40 miles through Lake Gatun to the lock of the same name. Here a series of three locks lowered the ship 85 feet. From there it was only a short distance to Colon and the Atlantic Ocean. We had traversed a total of 51 miles which took approximately nine hours.

By the time we arrived in Bermuda, we had heard of their famous rum and decided to check this out. The days were long and hot, and the drinks would be tall and cool. Once ashore we took a tour to a Rum Factory and purchased four cases (48 bottles) of Barcardi's light and dark rum, two cases of each. Since uncorking was not allowed until after we were back in international waters around midnight, I purchased an additional two bottles, which we smuggled aboard in our large handbags. You see, it was my birthday, and the party just had to begin before midnight.

It took another ten days to sail to London, and we supplied all our new friends with rum, including the staff. We partied continuously and enjoyed rum for breakfast, lunch and dinner without one hang over as we never skipped a meal and partook in every activity the ship offered, including ten laps around the deck after each meal. To our chagrin, we soon learned that we could only take one bottle each ashore upon arrival in England. We obviously would have many excess bottles. We solved this problem by tipping all waiters, room boys etc. with rum, with not a single complaint. Sadly, once ashore we had to limit ourselves to just one bottle each. The contest then began to see who could make her bottle last the longest.

Upon arrival in London, I picked up my brand new green Hillman Station Wagon, my transportation for the next four years in Europe. The first challenge was driving on the left side of the road in a strange, congested city, as my steering wheel was also located on the left. Obviously it was not a good idea to stay long in London, as it would be better to practice this foreign manner of driving on country roads. The real problem while driving was trying to pass another vehicle. I had to depend on Lillian in the passenger seat to tell me if there was oncoming traffic. We were very careful and very uneasy. We drove straight to Edinburgh for just a single day of sightseeing in that ancient city. We were anxious to press onward to Aberdeen, where we were greeted with Kathleen's smile, and, **so** *whits up the day!* (Hello!) She had returned home to live near her family after a two-year residence in Canada. Even though it was the middle of July, Scotland was a very gloomy and cold place that summer. Scottish homes did not have the luxury of central heating that I was accustomed to, and I spent my time in her parent's home bundled up in front of the fireplace not able to adjust my body temperature. *Lang mae yer lum reek!* (Lum being a chimney, and reek being the smoke going up the chimney, thus keeping warm and enjoying long life.) This toast obviously didn't work for me. Anxious to get away from that cold house, Kathleen suggested we take a tour of the Scottish Highland, and we readily agreed.

We packed up the Hillman and headed for Inverness and parts north to visit some of her relatives. Upon arrival we were offered the traditional cup of tea. We were astounded and amused as we sat and listened to Kathleen converse with her relatives, as we did not understand one word. Although Kathleen spoke our kind of English, it didn't take her five minutes to lapse into the Gaelic Brogue of Scotland - **Hoo are yi dayin?** (How are you doing?) She definitely had the Gaelic! So, to broaden our education, we learned that English is the official language of Scotland whereas Gaelic is the language of the Highlands and Islands of that Country.

Inverness is already part of the Scottish Highlands, so we decided not to go farther north. Instead, we went west to the coast of Scotland. I had previously heard stories of the Loch Ness Monster, which was first sighted in 565 AD. After that not much mention was made of this creature until 1933 when a couple camping along the shores of Loch Ness spied *"Nessie."* This was the beginning of the monster stories as we know them today. Earlier, in the same year of our travels, a one-man expedition decided to camp out to view the monster. He was successful in taking photographs of a large, unknown object which quickly descended to the depths of the Loch. We naturally kept our eyes out to spot *"Nessie"* as we drove along but knew such a sighting was rare. We were told that strange waves can be seen on the lochs most days, some looking like lines of humps twisting across the loch surface.

We didn't actually arrive at the west coast, as the land is broken up with a maze of lochs, making travel to the coast somewhat of a challenge. Our one disappointment was that we didn't get near any of the 787 Scottish Islands. Many are nestled along the Atlantic coast, with more belonging to island groups known as the Hebrides, The Orkneys, and The Shetlands in the far north. The worst incident on that trip was waking up one morning to find the Hillman stuck where we had camped along the shore. Not to worry as a friendly Scotsman soon arrived to the aid of the ladies!

Although I never warmed up while in Scotland, our drive down the west coast of Scotland while camping along the shore was amazing. By this time I had revised my initial impression of Scotland and thoroughly enjoyed the hills with the glens and dales of lush, unspoiled green scenery. The people were friendly in offering their traditional hospitality. Would I ever get back again?

Kathleen's time was limited and she so wanted to join Lillian and me on the next part of our trip, so we hurried back to Edinburgh. Here we watched as the Hillman was hoisted onto the ship. Then together, we four (yes, I include the Hillman), sailed away from Scotland through the *Firth of Forth*. **Gan awa i'l see yi later, dinna be long in coming back.**

Traversing the North Sea from Scotland, we soon landed in the port town of Bergen, Norway, **God dag!** *(Hello),* a city full of life and culture. We were first attracted to the vibrant fish markets along the docks as we had not seen the likes before. The old homes nearby were colorful, clean and inviting with the streets bustling with activity. Ascending directly into this little town were the cable cars that reached the mountain tops that skirted the city. The views were stunning overlooking the Norwegian Sea.

This was my first time in a non-English-speaking country, but Lillian was of Norwegian descent and had a fair enough knowledge of the language to get by. The first leg of the trip was a winding drive through the *Fjords* of Norway to Oslo. How pleasant it was to see the colorful, friendly Norwegians as they stopped their work to smile and wave at the rarity of a strange car with three young girls passing through their countryside. So here we were at last camping along the shores again and finding out that we could just be free and silly while enjoying the sunsets and colorful hillsides of this gorgeous countryside.

I guess that my strongest impression was how reminiscent the Norwegian Fjords, rivers and gorges are to the Fraser Canyon River in British Columbia, Canada, or even the drive north from Vancouver up Howe Sound to Whistler. The only difference is the many impressive waterfalls in Norway along the way.

Lillian had cousins in Oslo and was anxious to remake their acquaintance and thus make arrangements to stay with them for the winter after our European summer driving trip. We quickly drove down the west coast of Sweden and then to Denmark. We stayed in this fairytale country only long enough for me to decide that this was where

I would return to spend the winter and find work. It was sad saying goodbye to Kathleen after living with her a couple of years in Vancouver, visiting her and family in Scotland, and then touring parts of Scandinavia together. When would we ever meet again? In fact it was 16 years later when I returned to Aberdeen en route from Kuwait with my three-and-four-year-old children in tow. (We always kept in touch until her passing in 2009.)

By this time, we realized that our funds were very low, as we had foolishly splurged and sailed first class from Vancouver. So, we budgeted to live on the equivalent of $50.00 a month each by means of living in youth hostels and eating frugally.

The Continent Beckons

*A*fter all these years that first summer is somewhat of a blur as I only remember some of the fascinating countries and towns along the way and noting that I should return wherever and whenever I could. It seems that at that point we were anxious to do it all at once and focused on getting to the European Continent. Our whirlwind tour that summer included Scotland, Norway, Sweden, Denmark, the Netherlands, France, and then continuing as far south as Spain and Morocco.

Great Britain and Europe were not the medieval lands I had imagined before leaving Canada, but a wonderful exciting adventure just waiting for us each day. We wandered throughout these countries wherever that little wagon would take us, picking up other passengers in youth hostels to help pay for gas and other car expenses. Our meager diet consisted of bread, cheap wine and cheap cheese. When the situation arose, we would glean from the vegetable fields along our route soon finding out that the corn grown in France is for cattle and not for human consumption.

Our itinerary was focused on finding youth hostels or campgrounds along the way. When this was not possible, or to save money, Lillian and I just slept in the Hillman in someone's field. Until then we were too lazy or tired to pitch our tent after a long day's drive. Our first use of the tent was in a campground in the *Bois de Boulogne* in Paris. Here we linked up with some of our shipboard friends. They were touring the continent in an old truck renovated into a rustic recreational vehicle, the outside painted in outlandishly colorful and amusing scenes. From here we could easily check out the *City of Lights,* Paris. The traffic was manageable, and I soon learned to manipulate the *détournés* (roundabouts). After a week or so of our Paris vagabond experience, our two vehicles caravanned south into Spain, and spent a month relaxing on the beaches near Barcelona along the Mediterranean Sea. After leaving France, we were so thrilled to get a complete meal in Spain for so little money that we couldn't bring ourselves to leave. However, as the summer days threatened to turn into Autumn, the boys returned to England.

Since we had come this far south our thoughts turned to exploring more of Spain. This time we ventured farther south through the countryside, staying away from the large cities and finally arriving in Algeciras on the Southern tip of Spain. From here we took daily ferry trips across to Gibraltar, a 1400 ft. high chunk of limestone rock. This narrow rock peninsula marks the strait of Gibraltar separating Europe from Africa providing the only link between the Atlantic and the Mediterranean. Although it is situated in the South of Spain it was ceded for all eternity to the British Crown in 1713. A bit of trivia - if you sometimes lapse into "gibberish," you are talking Gibraltarian.

From there we crossed the Strait of Gibraltar into Morocco. It was a nine-mile ferry crossing to arrive in Tangier. Because Morocco is a French speaking culture, I felt more at ease with the language. We were mostly interested in visiting the bazaars (covered market places) and *souks* (open-air markets). I especially wanted to explore the busy *Casbah,* an old, crowded, fortressed area of Tangier. Lillian just wanted to relax in our dingy hotel room, so I ventured out alone in the late afternoon, returning to a stall at the bazaar where the salesman had offered to be a guide. I repeated my interest in visiting the *Casbah,* so once I paid him his requested fee, off we went.

We entered a narrow passage into an unbelievable ancient heritage and exotic culture, a millennium away from Europe. Here we mingled with mountainous Berbers, Nomads, and Arabs. The uneven cobblestone streets were narrow, with stone buildings towering above us on either side. An occasional courtyard gave a hint of fresh air, but other than that it was an uneasy feeling of being trapped. I envisioned what was inside some of those closed doors and was told of huge, luxurious palaces, mosques and baths surrounding large courtyards. I did get just a peek into one. If I had been alone, I would have been thoroughly lost in the maze of streets and alleyways. That fascinating afternoon was a highlight of my trip, but I was later admonished by a worried Lillian as I was gone for hours. When I think back on the experience now, I realize how lucky I was to have returned safely.

From Tangier we drove about 200 miles south along the coast to Casablanca, passing small villages teeming with the activity of small bazaars. Men were wandering the streets trying to sell their live squawking chickens, their legs tied together by string. Camels in the fields were paired with horses; apparently they were good, calming working companions. We were so fascinated that we made inquiries about driving all the way to South Africa. Our ideas were suppressed by stories of robbers, kidnappers, and much worse, not to mention breakdowns. We did venture on south about another 75 miles to Marrakech, where the desert and Atlas Mountains meet. This was the end of a passable road and we were forced to turn back, but not before we explored the bustling city of bazaars and souks behind *La Porte D'Or* (the Golden Door) where the colors, smells and noises overwhelmed us. The riotous marketplaces sold various wares, including brass goods, luxurious carpets, engraved leather, and colorful caftans, to name just a few items. In the Moroccan pharmacies were magic potions, spices and perfumes. Later we found ourselves at the *Djemaa El-Fna,* a huge medieval square with lively entertainment, the most appalling being the snake charmers toting their cobras in small baskets.

We didn't feel all too safe in this Berber-Arab-Spanish-Portuguese-French melting pot, so our short stay soon came to an end. There was so much more to see as we headed north again past the red-earthed landscapes of this palm-spotted desert.

However, it was then time to head back to Scandinavia for the winter. Lillian had her sights on returning to Oslo to live with some of her newly-found relatives and I had already chosen to spend the winter in Copenhagen.

Ma'a Salama! ... Peace be with you ..... Goodbye.

Denmark - God Dag ..... Hello

During the next several months of winter, we worked to save for the next summer's trip. For this, I rightfully had chosen Copenhagen, the delightful fairy-tale city. Traveling around Europe that first summer, I became accustomed to living in youth hostels and learned that those in Scandinavia were among the best. So I sought out a large, charming, modern, busy, youth hostel on the outskirts of Copenhagen. It was situated along a large lake, or was it a huge pond, with a ten-foot-chain-link fence surrounding the property. Inside the hostel were long sleeping dormitories, a common kitchen, and a dining/recreation room. I looked forward to making new friends here and finding a job for the winter.

My stay in the youth hostel was short. I do remember the Wednesday evenings, however, when we were allowed out later than the normal 10 p.m. curfew. The *Père* (Guardian) of the youth hostel would call a taxi or two and send us out for fun on the town to his favorite place, the lounge at the top of the Tuborg Brewery. Here we could party and dance, staying until closing around midnight. Every week upon returning to the youth hostel, however, we would find ourselves locked out with the fence securely chained. As boys will be, there was always one who would scale the ten-foot high fence, run down the long path to the hostel and throw rocks at the window where he knew the *Père* was sleeping. Eventually he would emerge sleepily grumbling that he had forgotten we were out for the evening.

Soon after arriving in Copenhagen, I remember sitting with some of these new acquaintances in a coffee shop just across the street from the famed *Tivoli* Gardens on *"Vesterbrogade,"* a main pedestrian

Bonjour Paris

Lillian was still not ready to join me, and I had already quit my job in anticipation of our summer trip together. My next thought was to drive straight to Paris on my own, as my time would be better spent in pursuit of expanding my knowledge of the French language. Upon arrival in Paris, I immediately went to the *Alliance Français* to inquire about classes but found the cost too steep for my budget. Luckily I was drawn to the bulletin board in a hallway where I found an ad posted by a young couple asking for an *au pair* to care for their infant son. They did not speak a word of English, so this experience would be more valuable than sitting in French classes. They were delightful, and that same evening I moved into their nearby extra apartment. In 1961 finding an apartment was nearly impossible so they had retained their smaller dwelling when they made the move to a larger one. They were both *coiffeurs* in a high-end salon near *L'Eglise de la Madeleine* in central Paris. They would be gone long hours each day. My days were then spent as a *parisienne* nanny, walking my infant charge to a lake at the *Bois de Boulogne* in the *16ème arrondissement* (district,) and sitting on a bench along with the other nannies. Back at their apartment I was not allowed to do any housework or cooking. When the young *coiffeurs* returned home each evening, they would get busy in their galley-type kitchen and soon present a most nourishing meal .... *à la parisienne.* Then we would sit and laugh and play well into the evening until time for me to return to my cozy apartment.

Time passed quickly, and Lillian sent word that she would soon be joining me. Before her arrival I needed to renew the English license plate for the Hillman, and my new family took it upon themselves to help me in this endeavor. They went to great lengths to cut through the red tape. Ultimately it

was decided by all, that since I wouldn't be returning to England with the Hillman and would only
continue through the European countries, I should
simply remove the existing plate. Somehow I found
a plate to replace it with the word **CANADA**
boldly printed on it, and with this we continued
our travels.

Upon Lillian's arrival, we decided to take some
time to enjoy Paris. One evening we went to a
sidewalk cafe in the heart of Paris and sat there
until a very late hour. It was a long way to the outskirts of the *Bois de Boulogne* where I still had the
use of the apartment. We hopped a metro line but
were unaware that at one a.m. this form of transport ceased. It was still a very long way home, and
our only alternative was to walk. We were soon
aware that someone was following us. Our natural
instinct was to try and put him off our trail. We
became more fearful as we approached the last few
blocks near my apartment ducking behind cars in
hopes of shaking off our pursuer. Finally we ran
into the building, quickly entering the cage-type
elevator in the middle of the spiral staircase. As
the doors closed, an arm came shooting through
the cage, causing us to let out tremendous screams

as the elevator rose to the third floor. We were now safe but extremely frightened even when securely locked inside the apartment. The next morning as we boldly stepped out into the fresh air, the apartment concierge yelled " *il vous a servit juste de sejourner dehors jusqu'a les petites heures du matin.*" (It served you right to stay out to such a wee hour of the morning.)

Au Revoir Paris!

The Mediterranean

We headed straight to the *Côte d 'Azur* in France. Always seeking the unusual, we soon found a camping spot clinging to the edge of a cliff at the seaside resort of Cassis, just south of Marseille. It was impossible to tear ourselves away from this paradise. We spent an entire month swimming and basking in the sun while lying along the rocks on the edge of *La Mér Méditerranée.* The highlight of our days was the descent down among the rocks to the sea below. Here we would snorkel the hours away, often spearing baby squid for our evening meal. We soon found out that these tiny sea creatures were extremely tough eating and by necessity learned that if we bashed them against the rocks for some time, they would become tender enough to place on our open campfire. This truly became the delicacy of *Côte d'Azur* living.

Traveling ever closer to Italy, we often camped right on the beach where we met many interesting campers with similar interests. On one occasion, we spent a couple of uncomfortable nights sleeping on the sand without our tent. Eventually an elderly lady approached us, stating that she was living up on the hill and had been watching us. She wondered where we would be heading next. Upon hearing that we would soon be heading towards Nice, she suggested that we stay in her rented villa until such time as we felt like continuing our travels. We were very thankful for this offer, as we were in much need of shower and bathroom facilities, not to mention a stove to make a proper cup of tea and light meals. Besides, we still had the wonderful beach and sea below our doorstep.

During our few short days enjoying her meager accommodations, we learned that she was doing exactly as we were. She would travel whenever and wherever the whim took her. Because I have forgotten her name, I will now call her Marie for the rest of this tale. Marie came from Paris and earned her living by allowing various *coiffeurs* to experiment on her hair. She had been permed, bleached, curled, straightened, colored and stripped along with other procedures. The little hair she had left was dry, scorched and straight, resembling a scared cat. Nevertheless that was her livelihood, and we found her to be a happy, eccentric lady. She confided to us that she traveled by hitchhiking and that invariably it was a man who gave her a ride. Regardless of his age, or her advancing age, he would soon ask her to sit a little closer, after which time his hands would wander to touch her boobs and legs. It was so amusing to listen to her along with her hand gestures that only the French can manage. We could not help but to take pity and warm to this adventurous lady.

We soon continued our drive along the coast with Marie sitting happily in the back seat of the Hillman. We wandered along thus, enjoying the beaches and the wind-swept glorious days of the *Côte d'Azur.* Lillian and I would, as usual, sleep securely locked inside the Hillman while Marie cheerfully stretched her sleeping bag alongside the car, undeterred by the dangers that we assumed to lurk outside. We would awaken each day with her playfully prancing outside just waiting for our day's adventure to begin.

Out of necessity, or perhaps a little mischievousness, we continued gleaning whatever field vegetables we came across to complement our evening meals. At first we were uneasy that Marie would frown at our prankish behavior but soon found that she hopped gingerly out of the car, not wanting to be left out.

This went on for several days while we thoroughly enjoyed our jolly French traveler. We eventually arrived in the tiny Principality of Monaco. We were headed to Italy and had given much thought about whether or not we wanted to be responsible for taking Marie into another country. Sadly, we gave her the news, leaving a very unhappy lady standing on the steps of the Monaco Palace looking back at us.

Au Revoir la France!

Ciao L'Italia

We had procrastinated for months about crossing the border into Italy due to numerous stories we had heard of the Italian men following and pestering young lady travelers. It was finally time to make up our minds and just do it if we were ever going to see Italy. The stories were true, as right there inside the customs office at the border were several young men presumably waiting for us with their flirting remarks. Luckily we quickly escaped and then drove quite a distance along the coast until we found a large campground on the beach. Thinking to outsmart the young *Italianos,* we pitched our tent on the sand under some trees; then, for a final touch hung our laundry on the lines outside, thus making it look very lived in. When nightfall came, we did as we had very often done before; we covered the Hillman windows with dish towels and settled in for a nice, undisturbed sleep inside. While we were safe, the tent was a source of merriment all night long as we heard the chattering, calling and laughter of young men surrounding it, and poking it with sticks, trying to get our attention. They never guessed we were safely snuggled inside the car. The next morning, while enjoying the beautiful beach, we met two Italians, an extremely handsome Alitalia Airlines steward and his companion, a very funny dwarf-like character .... not for me! Lillian and Graziano immediately took to one another, and we soon found ourselves traveling in a foursome towards Rome. I don't remember spending too much time in Rome that year as Graziano's family home was some miles north of the capital. There was a very narrow, steep, winding, one-way-dirt path that my Hillman precariously maneuvered to his tiny village way up in the hills. We were invited to spend time with the family and villagers of this extremely remote hillside community.

There was one store sparsely stocked with a few necessities, a humble church, and a few ancient, cold-looking-stone houses for the inhabitants. This was their entire world. It appeared that only a few young men ever made it off that hillside. Inside Graziano's home was a large, dark, cave-like room with a huge fireplace serving as their cooking stove and their heating system. This stone abode was indeed very cold but their humble hospitality was friendly, warm, and sincere.

Graziano had to be knowledgeable in a language other than his own in order to work as an airlines steward. He spoke Italian, some French, and a basic smattering of English. When we all met, I became the translator with my limited high-school French. Lillian only spoke English so she and Graziano conversed in a comical combination of what I called Franglish, or Franglais as it is more correctly named.

A short time after our arrival in Italy, Graziano was transferred to Geneva with the Airlines. Lillian and I, still wanting to continue our European experience, left Rome, but not before we threw our few pennies into the *Fontana di Trevi* to assure our return.

A piu tardi! .... Later

Venice

Venice

The attraction this time was Venice. The Hillman headed straight north, where we spent only a day or so at *La Serrenissima,* the most serene one, as Venice is also called. We wandered the narrow streets along this city of canals, crossing over and over the multitude of bridges. The well known *Ponte dei Sospiri, or* Bridge of Sighs, over the *Rio di Palazzo Canal* was a favorite. Lord Byron had popularized the belief that the bridge's name was inspired by the sighs of the condemned prisoners as they were led through it to the executioner. The bridge was built in 1600, connecting the Doge's prisons to the inquisitors' rooms in the main palace.

We wanted to take a romantic gondola ride but chose not to do so as we didn't have anyone along to romance us .... *che peccato!* ....what a shame! In our wanderings we didn't stray far from *Piazza San Marco,* San Marcos Square; only visiting *Basilica di San Marco,* St.Mark's Basilica, and an enticing glass shop nearby. At that time we didn't know about the island of Murano with its magnificent glass factories which have been in existence since the 14th century. Also unknown to us and thus missed was the *Teatro Ia Fenice,* the Venice Opera. This brings to mind *"trascorrerremo,"* my favorite Italian word from the opera, *La Traviata.* What a romantic way to say, "Let us run away together."

Only recently while reading a few books on Venice did I become acquainted with the *Palazzo Docale,* the Doge's Palace, even though the Palace is located along the canal adjacent to the *Basilica di San Marco.* We missed so much of the sinking city that year. It left a lasting impression and opened the door to interesting reading over the years. Another pleasure lost to us that year was the regional chilled glass of *Prosecco,* a dry sparkling wine .... *che peccato ancora!* This trip sparked an everlasting interest. I recently returned for a more leisurely visit.

Arrivederci Italia!

Yugoslavia

We were enthusiastic about driving into Yugoslavia, having been enticed by stories of other young travelers. Our thoughts were to possibly continue as far as Greece, which we didn't. In our eagerness we wanted to see it all! We were amazed, driving along the jagged Dalmatian coast, to view, by our count, as many as thirty islands clustered near the coast in the Adriatic Sea between Triest and Dubrovnik. In reality there are almost 1000 islands and reefs tucked along that coast. In sharp contrast to the extremely passable Italian *autostradas,* this road was wide and well banked curving in and out along the coast - a true pleasure to drive. This part of the country seemed to be well traveled, mainly with German tourists seeking out the many camping grounds. Our tour and the road ended in Dubrovnik.

When we stopped at a small country grocery store for supplies, we found several Yugoslavians surrounding the car as we left the store. They were excited and chattering away pointing to our Canada license plate. Somehow, we finally understood that they wanted us to follow them home. This we did and as we entered their large yard we saw a young boy run to get a neighbor. It turned out to be a retired sailor approaching us with a wide grin from across the yard yelling "What the hell do you girls want!" This surly stranger turned out to be our translator. We entered our new friend's small kitchen/family room, where we were motioned to sit down around the table. We found it strange that the men would sit down at the table with us for a meal, while the women remained standing behind, all the time touching and stroking our shoulders and hair. It was a very uncomfortable experience for us! We learned that it was the custom for the men to be waited on first by the women before they would themselves sit down for a meal. We also learned that this family had some long lost relatives in Canada and hoped that we would be able to reestablish contact for them.

Again my little Hillman was of great interest. A young couple in the family were having their infant son baptized the next day, and the father wanted to know if he could drive my car to the church for the ceremonies. We were of course invited to attend. I hesitated and finally agreed. So leaving our campgrounds early the next morning, we joined the family to drive together into a nearby quaint little village. I wasn't familiar with the denomination of the church, but later surmised that it must be Orthodox. It wasn't the free standing church that I was accustomed to, but instead attached to other buildings in a town square, with nothing more than a cross over the front door to indicate that it was a church. There were no chairs or benches inside, but instead little nooks around the perimeter, each permitting only one person to stand or lean. The church was small and dark. We didn't understand the ceremony at all, just the strong scent of incense, a few tinkling bells, and the fact that the young parents were proud and overjoyed.

A huge feast followed back at their house. On this very special occasion they had killed the turkey that the children chased around the yard the day before. We hadn't seen any other fowl on the property, and that told us how important this day was to them.

The next morning, it was time to head back north again. So, after bidding a heart-felt farewell, we chose an inland route, eventually arriving in Zagreb. By now one ancient city resembled another, so we stayed only long enough to attend a town market where we enjoyed the local music. The merriment inspired me to buy a hand-carved wooden flute. What a joyous experience. Soon it was time to leave Yugoslavia.

Do videnja Yugoslavija! .... *Goodbye Yugoslavia!*

Austria and Germany

I don't know why we didn't spend more time in Austria during our travels that summer. We meandered through that fairytale country with its colorful, tidy towns surrounded by rolling hills, fertile, well-tended fields and majestic views of the Alps. On one occasion we were crowded off the road by a parade of cows colorfully adorned in ribbons and bells. Obviously the cows had the right of way.

I have always regretted not stopping in Vienna, but we had so much more to see yet that summer and didn't want to take up the time in a large, busy city. Vienna would surely take up a lot of time.

I wasn't aware at the time, but very near our path was *Enns,* the oldest town in Austria. It was settled by the Celts in the Third and Fourth Centuries. It is situated on a river of the same name - a southern tributary of the Danube. Enns was my maiden name. The story was handed down to our family that a foundling was picked up on the banks of this river, thus our family name. It is still a dream to visit there someday.

We soon arrived in Munich, where our only interest was to visit a *biergarten.* Traditionally these are called gardens, since tall chestnut trees were planted above the barrels to keep the drinks cool. The *biergarten* we stopped at was not a garden but a beer hall nestled on a busy city street. Food was not served inside, so we parked right at the front door. We let down the rear door of the Hillman, spread out our own feast and enjoyed lunch, much to the amusement of passersby. Inside I was in awe at how many heavy beer steins a young waitress could carry in one hand. We limited our consumption to only one refreshing stein, and enjoyed what was more interesting, the gaiety and fun of that memorable afternoon.

Now realizing the musical adventure we missed in Vienna, we headed straight to Berlin and the

Komisch Opera - Berlin Musiktheater in East Berlin. This opera house had been damaged during WWII and further destroyed in 1945 with a reopening in 1947. Up to this time, the West Berliners were able to cross freely into East Berlin to attend the Opera as well.

Since we had taken the *S-Bahn* (suburban train) from West Berlin into East Berlin the previous year, we didn't think twice about re-entering the East now. One of our traveling companions that first year was a young boy with a Slavic name. He was afraid to make the journey over the border with us, so he didn't. I thought about the Slavic name I was born with, but that name was not on my passport, so I had no fear and was eager to make the short trip. We did a little shopping in the few sparsely stocked stores, as the prices were so ridiculously low. My treasures were three classical music records (this being the only choice in the store), which I cherished for years until they just wore out. My other purchase was a hideous wool, orange-and-black-plaid skirt that kept me warm for the next few years of European winters.

The streets of East Berlin were wide with buildings well spaced out among the vast, open, bombed out areas. Finding a restaurant was not easy, but once we did, we found the selection very meager.

Now on this second visit to East Berlin our focus was on attending a performance at the elaborate *Komisch Opera* that we had missed previously. This time we did make it to a performance, but after all these years I can remember only the elaborate interior of the building from our balcony seats. It was here that we met four American servicemen. As always in our travels throughout Europe, we asked if they had a commissary and cafeteria nearby where we could indulge in all those American foods we craved. They suggested that we join them on a picnic the next day at a lake. They promised to pick up the supplies. Our order was for chips, hot-dog buns and wieners with all the fixings. We asked them not to forget the marshmallows to roast over the fire. The next morning, as I am always the skeptic, I suggested to my five traveling companions that we hide our valuables and money under the floorboard of the Hillman station wagon and lock it. My reasoning was that we really didn't know these servicemen, and it was prudent to be on the safe side. We caravanned farther into East Germany, finally arriving at a huge lake surrounded by a sandy beach. It was necessary to leave our cars at a parking lot and then walk a distance through the forest to reach the camping spot. We pitched the tent just as a changing convenience so we could swim in the lake. A bonfire was made, and by the time we came to roasting the marshmallows, some East German soldiers came out of the woods yielding long bayonets. Frightened, we ran into the tent and huddled around the central pole. They proceeded to slash the tent with their bayonets, luckily not reaching or harming any of us. Outside we heard splashing, as our clothing, shoes and food were thrown into the lake. They departed as suddenly as they had appeared. When it felt safe to exit the tent, we quickly gathered up our few remaining belongings and ran towards the parking lot. One of the gals had previously wandered into the woods and witnessed our predicament. She circled back to the parking lot only to see other soldiers breaking into our car. From this we surmised that we were held captive only until the break in was complete. Luckily most of our valuables were safe, I only lost my camera, which I had forgotten to hide. They had rifled through the suitcase of the one young man traveling with us, so he lost most of his belongings.

One of the American servicemen then drove back to their barracks and soon returned with enforcements. We were taken back to their head-quarters and questioned all night. By six a.m. we were told to get in the Hillman and drive back to West Berlin. We were not to stop for anything, as surely the East Germans would be watching us from the forest lining the road. They added that they would come looking for us if we did not arrive in West Berlin in two hours. Because I was up all night, I could not stay awake to drive. We all took turns, but no one was awake enough to continue so we locked the doors and the six of us sat upright and took a long nap. No one bothered us. No one came to look for us.

After this ordeal, we stayed a couple of days at a youth hostel in West Berlin. During this time, a few young East Germans, male and female, also staying at the youth hostel, told us stories of having to leave their families, knowing that they would most likely never see them again. Some had walked for days or weeks in hunger and fear through the countryside and forests until reaching safety. They all spoke a little English, were well groomed and extremely polite. We knew that someone was looking after them, and they were safe.

One week later, the Berlin Wall went up. The *Berliner Mauer* blocked East Berlin from the West from August 13, 1961 through November 9, 1989.

Lillian was still in contact with Graziano and wanted to join him in Geneva instead of returning to Scandinavia for the winter. As this was less than 300 miles south we turned that little Hillman around and headed straight in that direction.

In a small village along the way, two weary travelers stopped in a bar late one evening. Here we met a young German barmaid, Ingrid. After an hour or so she inquired where we would sleep that night. I explained that we usually pulled the Hillman into a farmer's field, locked the doors, and then slept cramped but safe inside. Thus she offered that if we waited until midnight when she was off duty, we could go home to her apartment where she lived with her parents. This we did, talking for hours inside her very comfortable room. Ingrid was a chef and told the story of several years of training to get her degree, but found it impossible to find a job, even with her expertise.

Wearing my orange-and-black-plaid skirt after
a long cramped night sleeping in the Hillman in
someone's field.

Remember, this was not that many years after the finish of WWII, and we found this same story throughout Europe, where young people poured their hearts out to us, hoping to establish a lasting friendship and possibly a connection to travel to America.

When Ingrid departed that evening she carefully locked us in the room ..... Hmmmm ..... should we be concerned? In the morning we were awakened to shouting coming from the hallway. Finally a very upset Ingrid came into the room, explaining that we had to leave immediately. So we quickly gathered up our belongings, and with Ingrid's help, scurried to the car with her parents constantly screaming behind us. Again we had to leave a very sad friend in distress. Apparently her sister had married an American serviceman who treated her badly, thus the parents reaction. They argued that we were US servicemen disguised as women.

Our experiences in Germany were not that favorable, so with this thought I said,

Auf Wiedersehen!....*until we meet again!*

Switzerland

I only spent a short time in Geneva, and then not wanting to impinge any further on the young lovers' privacy, I took to the alpine ski resort of St. Cergue. It is situated high above Lake Geneva, only a 30 mile drive from the city of Geneva. This area is known for its cross-country skiing and many hiking trails through the forest. Lillian decided to come with me for a few days. Upon arriving, we found a friendly but deserted youth hostel. Even though it was only early September, we just couldn't get warm, even after piling on every blanket we found in the dorms.

My interest immediately switched to finding a job in hopes of warming up in someone's home. The next morning, I was hired to work at René Sports, a ski shop. I had the choice of working in the shop or in their home above the shop. Knowing that my french was not that fluent, I opted to work in the family home preparing the family meals.

Since I had recently worked on that cruise ship in Scandinavia, I often made Danish *Smørrebrød* for their dinner. I guess this was amusing to them, as when they were absent for a meal, they always invited a neighbor or friend to enjoy my creations.

Other than working, there wasn't too much to occupy myself within these mountains since I wasn't a skier, nor a hiker. Besides I didn't have the gear for such pleasures. I would occasionally have a day off upon which I would take a trip down the mountain to Geneva. The clutch on the Hillman was being stubborn, so on these days some of the villagers would gather with me just before the steep decline and push the car until I could engage the clutch. How I ever got back up the mountain on those days I cannot recall. Eventually I was able to save enough money to take care of my problem child, the Hillman. I wasn't used to this cold mountainous climate, so by December I decided to return to my fairytale Copenhagen. I was introduced to a young Danish girl working for the butcher. As she was homesick and eager to return home, we teamed up to travel, arriving in Denmark just before Christmas to celebrate the holidays with our Danish families.

Au Revoir La Suisse!

Denmark 1962

*A*gain I was faced with finding a job. Immediately after the holidays, I went to visit my employer of the previous year. There was nothing available at his office at that time; however, by the time I arrived home that evening, I had a phone call from him. He had arranged an interview for me with a firm that marketed Norwegian Sweaters throughout Europe. I was to make sure that I would be satisfied and happy with the job in every way before accepting it. This was strange to my ears because back home in Canada, it was always the employer who checked out the employee thoroughly. At that time their office was located in Copenhagen but was moving 20 miles north to Hørsholm where I lived. All of their staff, not wanting to travel the distance, had already resigned; so I was it. I was hired as a bookkeeper but after the move had to take on all sorts of strange duties. The most frustrating and comical was the manning of the switchboard. Now I had learned some Danish the previous year but definitely not to the extent needed. Fortunately, the owner of the company did speak some English. He was a very understanding person and put up with my hilarious handling of the switchboard. I found the Danish people to be very accommodating and helpful, and somehow I got through those first few days until a trained switchboard operator was hired.

The sweaters, suits and dresses were knit piecemeal by ladies working as restroom attendants around the country. My benefit was acquiring a few of these fashionable items when they were pulled off the display shelves.

Hørsholm was a small town, and my favorite part of the day was a 15 minute drive to the office through lush-rolling-hill countryside. Every morning I would stop off at a bakery to pick up a large crescent Danish pastry which I would consume as my breakfast on the drive to work.

Our staff soon grew, followed with regular, almost daily visits from salesmen. It was a custom in Denmark at that time for these salesmen to arrive with a bottle of beer to set on each desk. It became a particular problem during the days leading up to Easter. Since the beginning of the 20th century the Danes have manufactured a brew called *Påskebryg* (Easter Brew), which is a much stronger beer, experimenting with different ingredients. This is introduced a few weeks before Easter each year to celebrate the religious period. That was fine, but there were often more than a few salesmen each day, and I was finding myself slightly tipsy during my drive home. I began my counter attack by introducing small cans of V-8 juice to my fellow employees, and after a time the salesmen caught on. Soon V-8 became the favored drink offered.

During the year, I had visitors from Vancouver, two brothers who had boarded in my parent's home during their university years. Together we took a trip to *Jylland* (Jutland), a large peninsula connecting Denmark to Germany. We drove from Copenhagen southwest through the island of

Sjaelland, (Zealand), the largest in Denmark. Upon reaching the coast, we took a ferry across to a small port near Odense, our destination. This was the home of Hans Christian Andersen, the fairy tale writer and poet. We were back in our childhood as we reminisced about some of his more famous stories. His works number 168, some of the well known being "The Ugly Duckling," "The Little Mermaid" and "The Red Shoes."

Back in Copenhagen I had a dear friend named *Komtesse* (Countess) Annelise. She was a trained Egyptologist, and I always enjoyed visiting her apartment with her private museum of digs. We were especially intrigued by the phalluses brought back from Egypt. We were too timid to question Annelise about her findings. We were only interested and amused at the various sizes.

I had the feeling that Annelise was the black sheep of the family as she never mentioned her parents or siblings. I had no indication that she ever visited them in their homes or at the palace, thus I had no opportunity to visit the latter either. We always met at the university or the party scene. There were evenings when we would return home in the wee hours, so Annelise stayed over and slept on the floor next to my single bed. My landlady always exclaimed, "You made the *Komtesse* sleep on the floor!" During these times, our social group consisted of the two brothers from Vancouver, a Norwegian girlfriend living in Oslo, Annelise and myself. We traveled back and forth to Oslo.

In the mid 1980's Annelise moved to Giza, in Cairo, Egypt, and devoted herself to her great passion, Egyptology. She lived a lonely, eccentric life. Sadly, some years later, Annelise disappeared without a trace. The family, along with the Danish Embassy in Cairo, and the Egyptian police investigating for many years, have found nothing to suggest that she is alive. It was not until the mid 2000's that the Danish courts arrived at their decision. The Lady is presumed dead. The mystery may never be solved.

Later that year the children in the home where I lived came down with the mumps. I soon found myself inflicted with the same. That was a rough winter as I had to quit my job due to complications. In the beginning I had a sleeping sickness (encephalitis or not) which kept me in bed and sedated 24 hours a day. Luckily I was up and about within a short time but under doctor's orders not to work for two years. Even in this condition my wanderlust could not keep me down. Off I went to Oslo to stay with my girlfriend and family. It was the oncoming winter that shortened my visit, as the cold Scandinavian climate was painful to my head. So back to Denmark I went. This time the doctor's advice was to go south, as he thought I would not be able to endure the trip to Canada alone. Besides, Canada had cold winters as well. There was no hesitation; my choice was to head for Rome. It was not my desire to leave Scandinavia at this time, but in reality I had no choice. How was I going to drive to Rome? It was my dear friend and landlady who came up with the solution. She found a driver for me by inquiring among her friends. He would be happy to drive me just for the experience of the trip.

Farvel Kobenhaven! ..... *Goodbye Copenhagen!*

Speeding South to Rome

Within days we were off. As most people know, traveling does not always go smoothly, and this trip was no exception. We traveled down the Autobahn in Germany where life was in the fast lane with no speed limits at that time. My driver took advantage of this new-found freedom, and I was petrified when he resorted to driving at speeds up to 100 mph. Well, my little Hillman was obviously not built for this abuse, and it wasn't long before the engine blew up. We were left stranded near a little town south of Stuttgart, Germany. Thankfully the driver and I parted at this junction, and I was left to deal with my inoperable car. The only possible solution was to order a new engine, which I was told could take up to a month to arrive. I wasn't too happy with this situation or being stuck in a small town in Germany. After I made the necessary arrangements with the garage, I departed by train to Zurich, Switzerland, where I spent the next month.

I found a delightful small modern convent in the center of Zurich where I had my own room. Meals were taken in the main dining room where, along with the other residents, we were asked to help by hand making Christmas ornaments with glistening straw. With not much else to do all day, I took to wandering the streets to explore the Swiss way of life. Christmas decorations were up all around the city, and I felt as if I were in a story book as the store-window decorations were the most exquisite I had ever seen - and still to this day I have not seen the likes. Thanks to my broken-down Hillman, I had to satisfy myself with just window shopping, which was a delight and a Christmas gift in itself.

By the third week in December, I was able to pick up my newly restored Hillman. Driving myself this time, I continued on south, quite content being on my own while passing through the breathtaking scenery and quaint villages of Switzerland.

It was the 22nd of December before I reached Milan, where I felt I should find myself lodgings to enjoy the Christmas holiday season. I soon settled in an apartment with a *Signora* who rented out four of her rooms. We spoke a hilarious combination of French with a smattering of a few Italian words that I had previously picked up. She called me *Signorinalina* (the prettiest name I ever had). At that time I went by the name of Aline, the french equivalent of Eileen, my legal name. Milan was a good place to get lost in the winding Italian streets; I needed more.

Christmas day came, and I found myself all alone sitting cross-legged on my bed in my small room with nothing but a few magazines to read. I had kitchen privileges but no food. So I wandered out on the cold, lonely, gloomy streets in search of anything that might look appetizing. Eventually I found a small pizza shop where I had to endure the uncomfortable stares from the few male patrons as I entered the shop. My only thought was to get out of there as quickly as possible. So I took my burnt pizza - yes I remember it was burnt - back to my room where I wallowed in self pity, hoping the other renters would return that same day, which they didn't.

On the brighter side, I had received some Christmas money from my dad. I decided to treat myself to *Teatro alla Scala,* the Milan opera. This I did every evening between Christmas and New Year's. Residing in another room of the apartment was an Italian lady who lived in Caracas, Venezuela. She financed her trip home each year by bringing back Venezuelan furs to sell in Italy. She insisted that I couldn't go to the Opera without a fur, so off I went to La Scala each evening elegantly attired wearing a different fur. I felt like a princess, but a princess *sans chauffeur.*

By New Year's Eve, all the tenants were back at the apartment. We planned an evening together playing card games. Each one offered a holiday food treat, and I was glad that I had my Canadian fruitcake from home to offer. We were living on the fourth floor of the building, which I mention because at midnight the window to the street was flung open and everyone threw out their discards of clothing or whatever. I was sad that I had nothing to offer as the street people were out there waiting for this Italian New Year's custom. In reality it is a medieval habit to throw refuse out the window on New Year's Eve. The custom is still carried out to this day, but more often outside of the larger cities. The next morning with the holidays now being over, I decided to continue south to the warmer climate of Rome.

Once I loved a Roman 1963

It was the second of January, 1963, when I drove into Rome, *The Eternal City of seven hills*. Initially I stayed in a convent on top of a hill somewhere near St. Peter's Square. This was definitely not my lifestyle, however, as I was not about to be cloistered.

By this time, my dad had agreed to send me $50.00 a month for living expenses, ample money in those days. I found a room in an apartment which, as in Milan, I shared with a few other renters. To fill in many lonely days, I would wander the streets of Rome, putting in many long days just fascinated by another magical world opened up to me. I needed to find something of interest to occupy myself as I was soon feeling guilty about the money I was receiving gratis each month. My next step was to find a job that wasn't a job. That wasn't hard to do. I found myself living this time in the maid's quarters of a movie director's apartment. My job was to cook meals and get the apartment into squeaky-clean shape before his wife would join him from the States. There was little cleaning to be done, however, and I again found myself mostly alone and unoccupied. In reality, the draw was my Hillman again. My employer saw this as an oppor-tunity to use my vehicle for his purposes. Since he was using my car, I begged him to take me to visit the movie set one day. This he refused, saying that it was a different and rough world there, and as a young girl I would be subjected to being hit upon by the actors and the likes. So to this day I have still not been on a movie set.

Again, this was not working out; it was too boring. I soon found a position with the American Embassy as a tutor for the three children of an American Air Force Colonel and his wife. We lived in the fashionable district on *Via Cortina d'Ampezzo,* northeast of Vatican City. Again I lived in the maid's quarters, which were this time very ample; besides, I had no maid's duties to do. The colonel's wife, Jane, enjoyed the housework, which she did diligently instead of hiring a housemaid. I was told not to impose on her territory. I did offer to help their young son with his studies one day but found he was more knowledgeable than I. The two girls were equally studious and self sufficient. Thus I settled into a routine of occasionally cooking the family dinner, and once or twice that year I catered a large party at their home. I became Jane's constant companion, and since the children were almost teenagers, we were free to go on shopping trips, play bridge with her Embassy friends, take trips to the coastal town of Ostia, and even enjoy occasional trips to Naples, Amalfi, and the Island of Capri.

One of the more memorable happenings that Jane and I shared was the unfortunate passing of Pope John XXlll in June of that year. As the curator of the Vatican Museum lived in our apartment complex, he secured official invitations for us to the Requiem Mass held the 17th of June, 1963. We had seats right up front in the diplomatic section. One thing that is emblazoned on my mind from that day was the elderly Italian women wailing and physically rolling in the aisles in their sorrow. I still have possession of that invitation which reads, *"SEDE VACANTE Bigletto personale d'ingresso nella Basilica Vaticana per assistere alle solemmi Esequie che si celebreranno per Ia Santa memoria del Sommo Pontefice GIOVANNI XXIII, lunedi 17 giugno, alle ore 10."*

Other than my outings with Jane, I was quite free to continue my wanderings around Rome. It was late February of that year when I met my Roman. He had advertised for someone with whom he could practice speaking English. I had experience along this line, having taught conversational English to individual students while living in Denmark. It was the ideal ad to answer. I can still remember our first meeting as this handsome young doctor approached me in front of a sidewalk cafe in Rome near *Via dei Condotti* at the *Piazza di Spagna* (Spanish Steps). His half smile took me in, and we were immediate friends. I think that I was also immediately enamored. I hadn't remembered but I was recently reminded that during that first day we took a ride to the outskirts of Rome where we sat and talked. After that, we both eagerly spent quality time together.

Umberto had studied and received his medical degree in New York on a student visa after which he was required to return to Rome. He was a surgeon's assistant at the time. His English was impeccable, without a trace of an accent. I remember he told me that while in New York he would go through the English dictionary word by word. His vocabulary was vast and I can recall feeling inferior even in my own language. He was brilliant. He was distinguished, very tall, good looking, quiet, and very polite - always with an impish, mysterious half smile. In reality, I can't remember too many details of our time together 50 years ago. We wandered the streets of Rome as he showed me many of the fascinating sites and monuments. We went to interesting, inexpensive, out-of-the-way restaurants that a tourist might never find. Once again my Hillman came into play, as he liked to borrow my car. I willingly obliged, as I had the use of my employer's vehicles whenever I needed them. Later that year, we drove together to Lugano, Switzerland as I had to leave and reenter Italy to satisfy the requirements to sell my car in Rome.

The highlights of this trip north were two quaint fishing towns along the Italian coast. My favorite was the charming small port town of Portovenere north of Livorno in the Province of La Spezia. From here one can walk up the steep, rocky path to the castle and get a fascinating view of Portovenere below with its rows of pastel houses lining the bay and the Gulf of La Spezia, the gulf of poets. Favorites of many poets included Byron, Keats and Shelley. Across the bay, lay the picturesque town of Lerici. From here there are many level hiking trails to explore the small fishing villages along the coast.

Upon returning to Rome, I had no problem selling my reliable car, even though I only had a facsimile of a license plate which I had purchased in Paris with "**CANADA**" printed in large letters on it. Although our year together was always very pleasant, I sometimes wondered if Umberto's interest in me was in my car. There were also a few things he alluded to throughout the year which disturbed me - one being that he had a rush when a patient died on the operating table. At the time I dismissed that comment off as a joke. He also mentioned that God planned wars, floods, hurricanes, earthquakes and such as a means of keeping the population down. This was too much for my young mind, so I filed it away for future reference.

Still remembering that Americans and Canadians were always a possible link to North America was also a concern of mine, as Umberto's goal was to return to New York to work. His birthplace was at that time part of Yugoslavia, so in fact he held a passport from that country and not Italy, making it more difficult to secure a working visa for the United States. So another piece of the puzzle lodged in my mind was the fact that maybe this was his attraction to me. Besides, in the entire year I was never taken home to meet "Mama."

Rome had become my passion, but I was feeling guilty about staying away from my family for so many years. So, when my Father urged me to return home, I decided to oblige. Besides Umberto was obviously not in a position to ask me to stay, as young doctors in Rome at that time had little chance of advancement. I left Rome with mixed feelings in early December 1963, never looking back. It was a sad day when we parted at the Termini train station in Rome, he with his pondering, mystifying expression, and me with my pale blue sweater, which I knew he could barely afford. I wore that sweater fondly for many years until I finally had to give it up upon arrival in the tropics four years later.

Arriverderci Roma!

Back to Denmark

The train took me to Copenhagen for a brief reunion with my beloved Danish family. While there I was invited to dinner at the home of the auditor who often visited me at the job I held in Hørsholm the previous year. I remember at the time, I thought it strange that he would come to the office and sit and talk with me after working hours.

When I took that job in Jan. 1962, I was the only employee other than the boss, as the company had just moved from Copenhagen to Hørsholm, where I lived. We soon hired other staff including an accountant. I was the bookkeeper. Since I had worked in similar positions during my Vancouver years, I would usually say to him at the end of the month, "Aren't we going to balance the books?" Invariably he commented, "It's all right; we don't have to do it this month." I wasn't at ease with this answer so after a few months I did mention the fact to my boss.

Now upon my return to Denmark I finally understood that I had been under surveillance by the auditor as well. By this time the accountant was in jail and the auditor was apologizing for being suspicious of me.

Farvel København!

New York and the United Nations 1964

Before departing Europe, I took one last trip to Oslo, Norway, to visit my girlfriend. The ship I planned to take across the Atlantic departed from there. I was still not brave enough to fly, and the idea of sailing on the last voyage on the Norwegian ship, *Stavangerfjord,* appealed to me. Since it was already December, we had a very rough voyage. I was one of the few passengers to stay upright, as I found the only way to counteract nausea was to continually walk the deck. Our arrival at Pier 42 in New York City was a welcome event.

I set out to look for a job in this bustling city, as I was not about to move back to Vancouver. This was halfway between my home town and Europe. In my mind New York was the only solution. I checked into the YWCA and set out to pound the pavement. I was soon discouraged after finding employer's excuses, such as "You do not have a college degree. You do not have any experience in this country. You are not an American." Finally someone suggested that I try the United Nations, but I didn't at that point. I was supposedly hired as part of a ground crew by a small airline that flew out of *St-Pierre et Miquelon,* a tiny island south of Newfoundland, Canada, and a French territory. The idea of improving my french while working in a foreign culture was a fascinating challenge. The hire was out of New York, however, and to get my working permit I had to leave the country for a period of three months.

So then was the time to return home, which I did by taking the 2300 mile train ride from Montreal to Vancouver. I stayed with a girlfriend in downtown Vancouver and happily visited all my relatives and friends while revisiting my favorite places. I was surprised at the marriage of my mother eleven days after my arrival. I was not invited to the wedding. Our estranged relationship continued, and I rarely saw her after that.

I was glad when it was time to return to New York. I reported to the NY Airport about my job, but while waiting I heard stories from other employees that the *St-Pierre Airlines* had financial problems and employees were often just not paid. I couldn't afford to take a chance on that bit of news.

I went directly to the Secretariat of the United Nations and was immediately hired, based on the fact that I had recently lived abroad and had a smattering of some European languages. Having lived in different countries, they felt I would be able to easily adapt to the many cultures within the UN. I started work the next day in the payroll department.

I moved into an apartment with two other girls. It had one elongated living room, a small bathroom, and a very small kitchen. In the bedroom we lined up three single beds and had to crawl over one another to manipulate our way around. It worked like a charm with many laughs, even when we occasionally squeezed in a house guest from out of town.

One of these guests was a dear friend living in Hartford, Connecticut. We had met at the YWCA in New York City my first day there, and became lifelong friends. Christel had recently come from Hamburg, Germany where she and her family had suffered the ravages of WWII, often not knowing where the next meal would come from. In 1939, when she was four years old, her father left with the German Army to fight on the Russian front. She never saw him again, leaving Christel and her mother to fend for themselves. When Christel was in her early twenties she studied US geography and decided that Connecticut was the state she wanted to live in. At first she worked as a cook with a prominent family in Connecticut, thus my frequent trips to visit her on weekends. After a few years she sent for her mother, Mutti, to come from Hamburg to live with her. I enjoyed calling this fine lady, Mutti (Mother), as well. Christel studied hard and was eventually promoted to be the first non-attorney, advanced underwriting consultant at the Hartford Insurance Group ..... now Hartford Financial. She retired after more than 21 years, married, and moved to Florida where she and her husband reside today.

We didn't feel that Manhattan was a safe place to be out alone at night so we chose an apartment with a doorman and always took taxis. On the weekends I usually headed to Grand Central Station for the short train trip to surrounding states to visit those I had befriended. My favorites were Connecticut, Philadelphia, and Virginia.

After learning the payroll system at the UN, I was transferred to working on the payrolls of those experts working in the 114 countries around the world. I specifically worked on those whose contracts were terminating. We didn't have computers, only a tape adding machine. Payroll was paid out in three different currencies: one third in that of their home country, one third in the country where they worked, and one third in the US. Finalizing a termination was complex because of having to deal with many currencies. During the experts working term, many were upset as they had to pay into a retirement system that didn't pay out until the age of 60. The life span in some countries was only 55 or younger, so you can imagine their chagrin. With all this and more to check into, I only managed two payrolls a day. The next day it would all have to be double checked by another clerk.

During my time at the UN I had an amusing visit from some of my father's Mennonite relatives. We had visited them the year before while traveling by car from Manitoba, Canada, to Texas. There were several families along the route. All of these families were much disturbed that my dad and I were both single but lived 2400 miles apart. Back in New York, as I remained at work late one evening, the phone rang. The voice on the other end said, "This is your cousin, Marlene, from Texas, and we have come to visit you." There were two couples and an eight-year-old boy. I immediately went to meet them at their hotel on east 42nd street. When I arrived, there were only two persons waiting in the lobby and, upon inquiring, I was told the rest would be down soon. When they finally arrived they explained that they didn't know how or where to get off the elevator so they rode anxiously up and down until eventually the door opened at the lobby. The women were clad in their customary long-sleeved-black dresses buttoned up all the way to the neck. Black *babushkas* adorned their heads. The men were likewise garbed in the typical black *plain clothes* of the Mennonites. After supper at a nearby restaurant, we hailed a taxi as they were curious to see where I lived. I knew I had to keep them occupied the next day as I could not get off work, or, I am ashamed to say, did not want to. I explained how to take a subway down to the foot of Manhattan and then take a ferry to see the Statue of Liberty. After, each "little trip" they were to call me at the office. Next they were to take the bus back to 42nd Street and walk up 5th Avenue to Rockefeller Center to take the tour offered. They followed each direction dutifully, calling me after each mission was completed. Last on the list was a four p.m. visit to the United Nations' Visitor's Center. As I was well known in the building, I was somewhat timid of being seen with my well-intentioned visitors. So I arranged for a personal guide to take them around the various areas of that fascinating building. When I arrived at the visitor's lobby, I found the four elders sitting quite erect on a bench against the wall. The small boy was sitting cross legged on the floor facing the elevator, almost up against the opening doors. The tour went well for them, but unfortunately for me a co-worker had seen us and I was teased for months

They could now put aside their former impression that the UN building was so large that one has to use roller skates to get around it.

That evening, we had dinner in my apartment during a mini New York blackout. Nevertheless, we had a wonderful time sharing life's experiences, and it was good to count them as family. Upon their departure, I had the distinct impression they would return soon, but it was not to be as I soon left New York.

Life at the UN was very busy and did not end after working hours. Within the building were several little international eateries, bars and delegate lounges. The latter was off limits to anyone but the experts and delegates, but being young, my companions and I were usually invited in. Here we could mingle and talk to people from so many different countries and languages. Often times we would sit in at the UN General Assemblies.

I had always been interested in ballroom dancing, as this is what I grew up with as a young person in the large ballrooms in Vancouver. There was a group who would meet on the top floor of the UN above the Secretary-General's office during our lunch hour. Here we would dance, learn new routines and make new friends. Unfortunately I was reassigned away from NY after only a few months of this pleasure. Because of my love of opera, I liked to frequent the Amato Opera in the Bowery of Lower Manhattan. This little magical opera house had only 107 seats and was a place for amateur performers to hopefully be discovered. Of course I took in many theatrical performances along Broadway as well. Another favorite spot was the nearby Little Italy district. Just walking by, I could inhale the sounds and smells of the Italian cuisine and bakeries. How reminiscent of Rome. I was able to visit most of the NY sites during my four years there, the most spectacular being the view of the city from the top of Rockefeller Center. I think it is safe to say that my life in New York mainly centered around the United Nations. It was a good life.

During the latter part of 1967 I was offered a transfer to Panama, the Republic of Panama. Before departure I spent some time taking Spanish classes offered at the UN and then decided to take a freighter to Panama instead of flying.

Republic of Panama 1967

*S*ome believe the country was named after a species of trees, or it could mean, "many fish" or, "abundant fish." Or does the name come from the *Kuna* Indian word, *'bannaba,'* meaning distance, or far away?

The UN office was situated along the *Malecon,* a wide boulevard along the Bay of Panama. It took me half an hour to walk there from my apartment in a more local-flavor residential area of the city. This was done twice a day, as lunch break was two hours long. The Panamanians had a name for me, "Fula," meaning a tall, blond foreign girl, and I often heard this echoed as I went for my daily lunch walks. On one such occasion, I was stopped by a man begging for money. His story was that his daughter had died and he needed money to transport her back to their village for burial. I really had no money in my pocket, so he suggested we go together to my bank. Because it was just before payday, this was not a solution, so I bid him a sad farewell and continued on my way. Several months later the same man stopped me with the same story to which I replied, "You mean that you haven't buried her yet?"

We had a small office where I worked as an Administrative Assistant and Payroll Officer. I was in charge of those expenses incurred by the experts for different UN agencies stationed throughout Central America. I paid their project expenses and then made the monthly reports back to the individual agencies. Some of the agencies I worked with were, UNESCO (UN Educational, Scientific and Cultural Organization) out of Paris; WHO (World Health Organization) out of Geneva; a Forestry program with UNDP (United Nations Development Program) out of New York; and FAO (Food and Agricultural Organization) out of Rome.

One of my more interesting duties was to coordinate social functions for the experts visiting from other countries; this could be parties, dinners, sightseeing, or, most important, meetings.

On the theme of sightseeing, I arranged for several experts to go along with me to the *San Blas Islands* which lie off the North Coast of Panama, east of the Canal Zone. On 49 of the 378 islands and cays, one finds the *Kuna* Indians. The women make *Molas* using a reverse appliqué technique. They layer several colorful pieces of patterned cotton material and then cut and fold under to the color they want to expose. Then the edges of each cut are hand stitched down, leaving a beautiful design. On a better quality *Mola* the tiny stitches are nearly invisible. A typical design was a fish, and inside its belly a smaller fish. Red and black are typically the predominant colors, thus found on the top two layers. I found it interesting that they first made a blouse by creating two identical pieces of *Molas*. They then stitched the two pieces together, added a yolk and two puffy short sleeves of floral print, and rickrack. A *Mola* alone can take two weeks to six months to make depending on the complexity of the design. The tradition is that they cannot sell these without first wearing them. This traditional costume of the *Kuna* women is worn with a patterned,

Panamanian Molas

long, wrap-around skirt, a red and yellow heads-carf, arm and leg beads, a large beaded or gold neck piece, earrings and a nose ring. After the blouse showed some wear, the back and front *Mola* pieces were separated and sold to the tourists. A worn piece of *Mola* has more value. *The Molas* were often framed in a black wooden frame using black burlap matting. The *Kuna* Indians would not allow their photos to be taken unless they were paid $.25 cents for each person in the photo. At the time, I bought a few *Molas* for two US dollars each. They are now sold in department stores for up to $65.00 each. By the time I left Panama in 1971 the Peace Corps was teaching the Indians how to make ties, bathing suits, potholders, etc. out of their *Molas* - how distasteful!

A colorful, typical *barrio* (district) of Panama is a street named *Salsipuedes* referring to a congested, dangerous area meaning, "Leave if you can." It is one of the poorest areas of the city where one finds hundreds of Chinese merchants, as well as others, offering anything one could imagine. This colorful market place dates back to the 17th century.

The Canal Zone was very much of interest to me ever since I had sailed through it in mid

1960. In 1880 the French contracted to build the canal under DeLessups, builder of the Suez Canal. While the Caribbean offered no tide problem, the Pacific Ocean did. From 1880 to 1904 the French spent three hundred million dollars in an attempt to dig from the Caribbean side, achieving only a few miles. Yellow fever, malaria, and corruption brought that effort to an end. Meanwhile, Panama separated itself from Columbia and signed a 99-year lease of the Canal Zone to the United States. The plan was to utilize the 200 inches of rainfall by building a dam in the mountains to create a lake at about an 85-foot elevation. With a set of three locks at each end, the lake would provide enough water to raise and lower ships transiting the canal. It would also power the electric generators for all operations. Thus no pumps are required for the locks. However, the fresh water killed the barnacles from the ships' hulls, so pumps were required to remove them from the canal. Unlike during my trip through the canal in 1960, there was no such provision for residents to do so. We were only allowed to visit a viewing stand in the Canal Zone to watch the small locomotives called "Mules," guide the ships through the locks from that point.

In October 1968 I found myself in the middle of a successful *coup d'etat* against President Arnulfo Arias. I had taken a bus downtown near the palace to meet with a dressmaker, only to find the door boarded up and many soldiers yielding rifles in the streets. I was in the midst of turmoil and many glares and sneers saying, "What is this *Fula* doing in this part of town?" I quickly made my way back to the UN office. To my horror there were bodies being dropped onto the street from our office roof to the *Malecon* below. Our staff was scurrying around packing boxes and loading them into a truck. That day our office was moved from this riotous area to a single-story house in a very nice residential area. We had only two vehicles, a small Volkswagen for daily use, and a stretch vehicle for visiting dignitaries. Besides the office driver I was the only one who knew how to drive. For the next few days, we drove these two vehicles around the city. If left unattended, they could be bombed. At night, we parked in a garage under my apartment building, way in a back corner between two hearses. I was petrified to go in there. After a few days, the streets were quiet and vacant except for the occasional outbreaks around the city. The UN office in New York kept calling, asking if I would like to return to the US, but I declined.

In my spare time, to become better acquainted with the locals, I gave English conversational classes at my apartment for Panamanian business men and ladies. I also taught English at the Panamanian-North-American Cultural Center in exchange for Spanish lessons.

It had been years since I left France, so I also joined the *Alliance Française* for french classes. I sat in a class of Panamanians, thus improving my knowledge of both spanish and french. During my last year, I passed the stringent exams at the top of the class since my conversational skills were far superior to those of my classmates. For this I won a month-long trip to Paris to study at the *Alliance Française*. The Panamanian students were not too happy that a *Fula* had won a scholarship meant for their country. I was uncomfortable with the fact as well and since I had already lived in Paris, agreed that we would have a drawing for the top three students at the upcoming *Bastille Day* on *Le Quatorze de Juillet,* the 14th of July. I was relieved as well as disappointed that I did not win. In fact, I was soon to be married and could not be running off to Paris.

An expert, Bob Carpenter, from the FAO project centered in San Salvador, El Salvador, was my intended. I guess one could say I was his paymaster, as he had to come to me in Panama for money for his fisheries project. It wasn't easy to get a marriage license in Central America, as each county I had lived in had to certify that I had not been married there. Eventually we were married in San Salvador in the midst of another *coup,* making it unsafe to walk the streets, but that did not deter us. I guess that my spanish was not all that good as I can remember the pastor stopping the ceremony and asking, *"Usted entiende lo que sucediendo?"* Do you understand what is happening?

Adios America Central!

Our Wedding Announcement

Miss Aline Enns

and

Mr. Robert Charles Carpenter

Announce their marriage on Monday, the
fifteenth of

March

nineteen hundred and seventy- one
San Salvador, El Salvador

Our first home will be in

Manado, North Sulawesi (Celebes)

Indonesia

Mailing Address:

% united nations development
programme

P.O. Box 2338

Djakarta, Indonesia

Indonesia 1971-72

The next morning we boarded a plane for Rome, as Bob had to be briefed for his new project at the FAO headquarters. What a honeymoon - a two week visit to my beloved Eternal City, Rome, and a brief layover in Bombay before finally arriving at our destination, Djakarta, Indonesia.

Before departing for Indonesia in the spring of 1971, we heard that the population was upwards of 119 million. That was the most populous area in South East Asia. Sumatra, the larger island northwest of Java, is one of the East Indies that

Columbus sailed westward to find. We started out in the capital city of Djakarta on the island of Java, which alone had swelled to about five million citizens. These figures were staggering to us, because Java is such a small island, only 255 sq. miles.

Djakarta is located on the northwest coast of Java and has been the capital city of Indonesia since the Fourth Century. The Dutch had arrived in Indonesia seeking pepper about the beginning of the Sixteenth Century and prevailed there until Indonesia proclaimed independence in 1945. Years later, after Sukarno's fall in 1970, some Dutch businessmen were allowed to return. This new venture for us was a joint World Bank/ FAO fisheries project designed to increase the tuna and mackerel industry to world markets. We were actually to be stationed at Manado, the northeastern tip of the Celebes Islands, also known by its Indonesian name, *Sulawesi*. .... This is what our wedding announcement notes as our first home. Still we started our new life comfortably installed in a fashionable hotel in Djakarta, while Bob worked on the feasibility study for the project.

Our transportation – a Bejak and driver

Many streets in Djakarta were unpaved and muddy due to frequent rainfall and flooding. This made walking through the pot-holed streets unpleasant, so we frequently hailed a *Bejak* - a covered two-seated cart mounted on the front of a bicycle. These carts were so narrow that two non-Asian people like us had to each sit on one butt, twisting ourselves sideways so we could uncomfortably fit as we jounced along the streets. Eventually, after our departure from Indonesia, the slow-moving *Bejak* was banned from central Djakarta as a menace to the rest of traffic. True to our expectations the crowds were staggering with saronged women carrying their young, beggars holding their hands out with their pitiful cries, and vendors trying to hawk their wares. The Dutch had built a maze of canals winding throughout the city. This led to the repugnant odors that permeated the city because they were used not only for transporting wares, but also for swimming, a place to do the daily clothes washing, a place to bathe, to brush one's teeth, and to relieve oneself.

After a few months of being acclimated to our new surroundings it was time for us to continue to our destination of Manado. For this 1500 mile trip we boarded the Garuda Indonesian Airlines, with our first stop being at Surabaja, near the opposite tip of Java Island. Next, we flew to an airport half-way up the west coast of Celebes Island. Here while waiting the many hours for the next leg of the trip, we heard stories of the airlines having to ditch at sea, and the Indonesians not knowing enough to get out of the plane. To confirm this unsettling bit of information, a missionary related to us that he had at one time saved the passengers from this very fate, one they didn't deserve.

Some airports in Indonesia were commonly grazed by dwarf buffalo to keep the grass down on the airstrip. When a plane was due, a bicyclist was sent onto the runway to chase the buffalo away. This was also a signal for the passengers to get ready to check in.

When we landed at the northern tip of *Sulawesi,* we were still many miles from our final destination, Manado. We still had to travers this hot, humid, wild, mountainous tropical jungle by jeep. We found that my husband had to divide his duties between Djakarta and Manado during our two years in Indonesia. These trips were more frequent than I would have liked, as I am not a relaxed air traveler.

Our home in Manado was in government guest quarters. It was no more than a small building with a living area and a wooden table, a bedroom with a wooden bed, and a tiny bathroom. The shower flowed from above, gushing onto the floor and toilet. Bob would get up earlier than I in the morning to check out the bathroom to get rid of the humungous scorpions, before I sleepily wandered in. There were mornings when the goats would find their way into our bedroom and wake us with a lick on the face. These were not our only uninvited guests.

Looking down the hill at Manado

Apparently, we were the first foreigners to move into these parts other than a missionary family some miles away whom these people had never seen. Down the hill was a small school and each recess and lunch hour the students would run up the hill and into our house to stare at these strange people. Of particular interest to them were the rings on our fingers, and our eyeglasses, which they would point to and touch all the while with a myriad of giggles. There wasn't much we could do with our new found friends but to enjoy their amusement and wait for the school bell to beckon them back down the hill.

We didn't have any cooking facilities, as a cook shack was located down the hill at the fishing docks. Our house boy would carry plates of food up the hill to us each morning, noon and evening, the best being the coconut fried whole fish. It wasn't long before I became seriously ill and I was in danger of losing the baby I was carrying. Luckily someone located a Chinese doctor some distance away who came to our little abode. He gave me an injection to stop the severe vomiting and cautioned that I had to be more attentive to what I was eating.

I started noticing more of what was going on in my surroundings. I had already taught the house boy to go into the bathroom to wash his hands before handling the food. When I followed him, I found that after washing he would reach into his back pocket and take out a filthy handkerchief and proceed to dry his hands. I was horrified, and this habit of his was soon corrected. Then, after a meal he would take the empty dishes and climb a ladder up the water tank to wash the dishes. This disgusting practice was also stopped short as this was our drinking water as well.

The fish was definitely suspicious, but we were in this country to promote the fishing industry so

what should we do? We knew there was no refrigeration down at the dock side so we exercised the
following steps. After the morning meal we would
break off a piece of a fish fin and send the plate
down the hill to the cook shack. At noon the same
fish returned with its broken fin so we broke off
another piece and again that plate went down
the hill only to be returned for the evening meal.
Out of necessity, we took the drastic measure and
stopped enjoying this most delicious course. This
is when I started with extreme measures, buying
from the local market a dish pan, a dish rack, dish
soap, a kettle, a couple of cooking pots, a couple of
rinsing pots, and a small kerosene camping stove.
Hence I taught my dear house boy to boil the
water, wash the dishes in hot soapy water, plunge
them into near boiling water, twice, place them
in the dish rack and cover them with clean dish
towels. Oh yes, he was also to close all windows to
reduce the fly population. It became sweltering in
this limited space, and he was ringing wet by the
time he finished his chores. He never complained
to me. Later, he would take Bob aside and say, "I
no dirty boy; I no kill Mrs. Bob." I felt sorry for
him. He was then not to touch the dishes until

it was time to return to the cook shack with the sanitized dishes to collect the next meal. Before he descended the hill, I would make him wrap the needed dishes in the clean dishtowels. Obviously fish could no longer be an option for us, but I still couldn't resist their coconut fried chicken and took my chances. I insisted that he only bring us soups that I could re-boil, raw eggs which I cooked myself, and their most delicious homemade bread as I could slice off the crusts where the bugs would settle. I allowed fruit with their skins on, and I can't remember a thing about vegetables, if any. I soon started feeling well, and my baby boy survived. I think the locals are still talking to this day about that strange, sick woman.

We took other measures as well to make ourselves more comfortable. We soon put a lock on the door to keep the children and animals out. We bought sheets of screen for the windows. With the scraps of leftover screen, I handcrafted some crude fly swatters, much to the amusement of our help.

If we were to endure these accommodations for the better part of the next two years, we decided that we would be better off building our own house on an adjacent property. This two-story structure was soon framed, but plans changed as we were soon to return to Djakarta. We often wonder if our house is still there or ever finished. We will never know.

While still in Manado, we took evening walks down along the docks where the fishermen would huddle, squatted alongside the boats to tell tales of the day. At this point, they were not doing much fishing. Instead they were trying to get a tired fleet back to being sea worthy. I was more interested in what facilities might be in this small community. The streets and yards were clean, as they were swept each morning, the custom in most of the Pacific. I was amused that they would sweep the dirt with a broom. The wooden houses were small and neat. As we strolled the lanes among these homes, the people would come out to greet us, often inviting us in for tea. I had to be polite, but with my experiences up the hill at our guest quarters, I was cautious and would just sip a little tea and forego any other refreshment offered. On one of our walks in our tiny village of Manado, we came across the maternity barn. It was a large wooden building with loose siding allowing the wind to blow through the slots. This also allowed curious locals to amuse themselves by peering in when patients were there. Inside we found plain wooden beds with no facsimile of a mattress and no sheets or pillows - just wooden slats to lie upon. When I asked about anesthesia, our guide was astounded at such a thing and said that women would just hang onto the headboard for pain control .... this is pain control! Of course, just from the looks of the outside of this barn building, and the lack of a nearby doctor, I had already decided this was not where I would give birth. I was just as curious as the locals.

Years later I was asked how we kept up with local and world news. Well, we didn't. There was no written material to be had, not even a radio. Our only contact with the rest of the world came by word of mouth from our missionary friends. We were completely cut off from the modern world and only a rugged jeep trip to the airstrip and a perilous plane trip to Djakarta would get us back to reality.

Previously, back in Djakarta, I had visited a clinic for the required pregnancy blood tests. The needles were 1/8 inch wide scoops resembling the shape of an extremely narrow pinky fingernail. I was told these had been around since WWI. After that experience we sought out and purchased our own sterile, sealed in plastic needles which accompanied me everywhere. It always bothered me when medical personnel were so delighted to use them, and then ask to keep them. They would then wash and reuse them on other patients.

We found that Bob's duties would require him to work in Djakarta for some time, so back to the comforts of the hotel we went. We moved back to the second floor, the only floor completed, even though construction had been under way for years. This was evident by the dark and dingy hallways and rooms. Eventually the fifth floor was complete, not the third nor the fourth, but only the fifth. So just a short move upwards and we were in luxury.

Small rumbling earthquakes were almost a daily occurrence in Djakarta. While on the second floor of the hotel we could easily make our way slowly down the one flight of stairs and out onto the street until we felt it was safe to re enter. I found two problems with the fifth floor. First, I was now very heavy with child and, I couldn't make it up the elevator to the fifth floor without becoming terribly nauseated. As the doors opened,

I would dash to the bathroom in the first vacant room I could find. Also, during an earthquake, it was impossible for me to get down the five flights of stairs and out of the building quickly. Needless to say, within a week we were back living on the dingy second floor again.

Bob frowned on any show of extravagance and believed that we should instead blend in as much as possible with the locals. Therefore, we did not drive a car, and I did not wear expensive jewelry. He dissuaded me from joining the American Women's Club, although I did sneak off to a meeting or two, as their tips on living in Indonesia were invaluable. Instead, I linked up with several Indonesian women who were the wives of the government officials with whom Bob dealt. I was amazed at their grace and kindness, and definitely at their colorful attire. I think that their interest in us was a mere curiosity.

1972

The time for the birth of my child was nearing, and we had already made arrangements for me to depart for Singapore, where I would share an apartment with a Chinese/German couple.

Airline rules dictated that I could not fly past my seventh month. The timing was convenient, as another FAO expert was just finishing his term in Singapore and would be vacating his room in the apartment mentioned above. Upon arrival at the Singapore Airport, I was pulled out of the security line and told that I could not enter Singapore for the purpose of birthing a child. Where could I go now? It was finally decided that I could stay as long as I signed a document stating that my child would not be a Singapore citizen. He does have a Singapore birth certificate, but is a US citizen. I also inquired about his having a dual US/Canadian citizenship, but at that time infants born outside of Canada to a Canadian mother were not entitled to Canadian citizenship. Now if the father were Canadian, that would have been a different story. So I moved in with Sheila and Gunther, who are still to this day my dear friends. For the next month I had only to shop for the baby and dream up names. The elevator where we lived had a sign on the wall with the word *"Kimsea"*. *Since* the name Kim was on my list, I decided that if the baby were a girl, this would be just fine. I discussed this decision with some of the girls at the hair salon one day, and they were aghast! They explained that in the Chinese culture a name has to have a meaning and "Kimsea" was just the name of the elevator company. Luckily I gave birth to a baby boy and rightly named him Robert Arthur after his father and grandfather.

I spent two weeks in the Youngberg Adventist Hospital on Upper Serangoon Road in Singapore. Coincidentally, I was lucky enough to get a doctor who originally came from California and had gone to medical school with a cousin of Bob's. I say "lucky" since at that time few doctors recognized a condition called "placenta previa". Had I not had this dedicated doctor by my side, both my son and I would probably not be alive today. Bob didn't understand why I couldn't get out of bed even a few days after the caesarean without almost passing out. His philosophy was that people die in bed. This became such a problem that the doctor finally told him to go back to Indonesia and that when I was ready to be released from the hospital, he would personally drive me to the airport ..... which he did ten days later.

Apart from our few stays in Manado, we had been living a year in the hotel in *Djakarta*. By this time we realized that it would be at least another year before we could return to Manado as the feasibility study was not nearly completed.

Although the hotel we were living in tried to make us as comfortable as possible, this was just not a place to try to raise an infant. We found a detached apartment behind a large home, yet still very near to central Djakarta. We could still use the services of the *Bejak* for our transportation. Our new home was a series of rooms situated in an L shape, each opening onto a central courtyard. There were no doors between these rooms. In the corner of the L was the bathroom which just consisted of a toilet and a large cement square reservoir. From this we showered by dipping a bucket in and splashing ourselves. There was no such thing as a heating system, so we endured the cold-water showers. Washing hair was a particularly chilling experience.

We had a young maid who would squat in this square bathroom and wash our clothing and the baby diapers, all of which were hung outside atop of bushes, or just thrown on the small patch of lawn. I mean thrown, not straightened out but just thrown in a heap with little effort to spread them out. With this kind of treatment all the clothing needed ironing.

It was not the custom in Indonesia to give the maid a day off, as the Americans reasoned that a maid would travel to her family's home in the country for her day off and more than likely not return on time. Another reasoning was that a maid could be spoiled by giving her a day off, and this would then be expected from future employers. We found this system rather abusive, so we offered the maid one day a week off with extra money to go to the cinema, a luxury the local people just couldn't afford. The monetary offer was rejected as intended and she counter offered, saying that she would rather forego the movie and use the extra money to take a bus to school so that she would not have to walk the distance. How could we refuse? We knew that she was studious, as I often found her crouching under the ironing board trying to read a book. I had found the exact same thing with my houseboy in Manado. He would hide and squat in the strangest places so he could read. Books were noticeably non-existent in this part of the world, but he had acquired a textbook that had been translated into English by a professor at the University of Djakarta. I asked to see the book and was shocked that the translation was not clear enough to understand the English meaning. From then on, I spent hours correcting the grammar in his book while trying to keep the meaning as I understood it. Unfortunately we did not stay long enough in Manado for this to make a great impact on this young, eager student.

Years later as Bob and I reminisced about our days in Djakarta, I discovered that he was slipping the maid extra money for her studies as well. Kudos for her!

Selamat tinggal! ..... *Goodbye*

Republic of Palau 1973

*B*efore departing for Palau, we spent a few months in Redondo Beach, California, where my daughter Karina was born. Bob departed the US a few months before the children and I. I wanted Karina to be at least six months old before we traveled.

Palau was a territory administered by the United States under a Trusteeship Agreement from the United Nations since 1947. It is situated in the Caroline Islands of the South Pacific. It is 500 miles east of the Phillipines and 800 miles southwest of

Guam. It has eight prime islands and over 250 smaller ones. It gained independence in 1994.

Bob was hired by a Seafood company out of California and was charged with refurbishing the fishing fleets and encouraging the Palauans to get back to pole and line fishing. At that time, the US government was shipping at least one large container per month filled with cans of tuna for the Palauans. It was easier and more economical for them to open a can, pour it over a pot of rice, and thus feed an entire family.

We lived in a double-wide mobile home on Malakal, a small island south of the main island, Koror. It was reached by a short, narrow, dirt causeway. Our house was within the compound of the fish plant, the latter being surrounded by a ten-foot-chain-link fence. From the front porch, I could look out and see the small fishing fleet lined up along the docks. The fishing plant was directly across a large expanse of grass and the office was just to the right of us inside the main gate. A separate six-foot-chain-link fence enclosed our home. The fishermen liked to squat just outside the fence to watch our children at play in their sandbox and on their swing, as Palauan children had no such luxuries. There were banana trees on the property, and someone would occasionally cut down a banana bunch and hang it on our back porch. Under Palauan custom these were not our banana trees even though we lived on the property. I soon learned that they belonged to the locals who had planted them prior to our moving onto the property.

Since the one small local food store had limited supplies, it was a practice for a new plant manager to buy all remaining food supplies from the departing manager. This we arranged for, paying a few hundred dollars for the inventoried food. It took a few hours for the previous manager to travel by car and ferry to the airport on the island of Babelthaup and then for us to make the reverse trip. By this time the freezer at the house had been half emptied and the food storage units at the plant were equally half devoid of food. This was our welcome to Palau and our way of learning their custom of sharing everything.

Before departing the States, I had to make a shopping list for a six-month supply of food that was shipped to Palau by the company. We could only buy in case lots but soon found that it was easy to sell extras to other expatriats that had to rely solely on what could be purchased locally. Before the ship arrived, Bob had large, locked, storage cupboards built at the plant. Even so, some of these supplies were pilfered. Anything kept in the house also had to be under lock and key.

Palauan gardens were tended by the local women where patches of dead leaves and rotting fish nourished a root staple called taro. Banana and breadfruit filled in between. Taro is very prickly to the skin and one has to lather one's hands with oil to prevent this irritation. Deep fried taro slices made delicious chips. Coconut trees furnished other necessities including utensils, thatching, cloth and drink. Our maid, Suzuki, would sit on the back porch and scrape the inside of the coconut into slivers. This could then be strained several times in a cheese cloth making various strengths of coconut cream or milk.

Some of the common foods in Palau:

Taro is probably the most important starch food in the Pacific Islands. It is a favorite for Palauan feasts and in earlier days was regarded as a symbol of wealth. The tuber is most commonly used and may weigh up to ten pounds. The hairy, brownish skin is scraped off before boiling. The flesh varies in color from almost white, to grey, purple, or mustard shades, depending on the variety. The flavor is bland and sometimes has a hint of sweetness. There are about 100 varieties of taro in the world. Cultivation of taro is arduous work. In Palau women work waist high in black mud to prepare the soil for planting. It can be grown on dry land but that taro is inferior. Taro has a six month maturation period. With some varieties the leaves and leaf stems may also be eaten.

The *Banana* was discovered growing along the Indus River in India three centuries before Christ. In Palau they are planted in family gardens. They thrive in the humid climate, and the loose, well-drained sandy soil. Each plant bears between 50 to 200 individual fruits. Each bunch may weigh from 50 to 125 pounds. After the plant bears fruit it dies. The stalk is then cut down and another rises in its place from an underground root system. When unripe bananas are cut down, their outer skin is green and the flesh is white and almost tasteless. If eaten in this state they are some-what starchy and somewhat indigestible. When bananas ripen they become yellow in color and taste sweet. Bananas are generally harvested green. If they are allowed to ripen on the plant they lose their flavor. The color of the banana is a good hint as to the way it should be prepared. If it is tipped with green it should be broiled, baked, or fried. If it is all yellow the fruit is ready to eat fresh, but may still be cooked. In this latter stage it may be used in donuts, puddings, cakes or pies, etc. If the skin is flecked with brown the banana is fully ripe and mealy. Use this ripe stage in fruit salads, breads, cakes, or just good eating. The people of Palau use the green banana in soups, stews, or as a vegetable. They also mash the ripe banana and mix it with coconut milk. The banana leaves are useful to wrap fish and meat while baking in the oven.

Plantain, or cooking banana, is a larger variety. It is less sweet and more starchy than the ordinary banana. It may be fried, baked without peeling, boiled in water or coconut cream, and used for making delicious chips.

The *Coconut* palm is a symbol of the South Seas. It can tower to a height of 60 to 100 feet. It takes about six or seven years of growth before the palm will bear fruit. One palm tree produces an annual crop of somewhere between 75 to 200 nuts and continues to be productive for 60 to 80 years. For drinking purposes the coconuts are gathered by islanders who scamper up the long trunk disappearing among the fans of coconut bunches and leaves. The nut is chopped off with a small machete and dropped to the ground for gathering. The nut with its brown fibrous outer shell has three "eyes" which resemble the face of a monkey. The name derives from the Portugese word, coco, meaning monkey. From the "eyes" of the ripe fallen fruit, roots of a new palm will form and grow. The coconut consists of an outer covering or husk with the center cavity filled with a flavorless liquid. There is a white jelly-like deposit on the inside of the shell which can be scraped out and eaten, or, more often, fed to the chickens. At this stage the water of the green immature nut is best for the digestive tract. During the second stage, or drinking stage, the outer husk begins to turn olive brown. The juice then has a good flavor and consistency, and the nut has attained its greatest weight. When the nut is opened and drained, the meat inside is tough and chewy but flavorful. Finally the mature nut develops. In this third stage the exterior covering is brown in color, and becomes lighter in weight. Any remaining liquid is now strong and bitter. In this stage the meat is ready for grating or drying for copra, the dried coconut meat yielding coconut oil.

The coconut leaves are used for roofing materials, baskets, fans, brooms, mats, hats, handbags, wall screens, toys etc. The mid rib of the leaves are used to make needles, combs and skewers. The husk fibers are used to make cord, sennit, rope, nets, stuffing used in furniture, and matting. Buttons, ornaments, containers and fuel are made of the shell.

"If man were placed on earth with nothing else but the coconut tree, he could live in happiness and contentment".....An ancient Syrian saying.

Betelnut is the seed from the Areca palm tree growing in the South Pacific. The nut, with added lime, is wrapped in a leaf from the tree. This is chewed giving the effect of a mild stimulant. Medicinal properties include; as a digestive aid, an anti-inflammatory and a pain reliever for headaches, joints, and tooth-ache. It is also a known human carcinogen.

The marine **Crocodile** in Palau is consid-ered one of the most vicious animals in the world. It provides a tender and tasty edible meat. It is commonly roasted underground alongside a pig for feasts and tastes a lot like white chicken meat. Crocodiles are scarce and lurk in the Mangrove swamps.

There was a small vegetable market in Koror where outer-island villagers would occasion-ally arrive with their canoes laden with produce. This was set out on a table at the market. Since there was never enough to supply everyone, it was the custom to put a hand on the basket wanted, resulting in a maze of criss-crossed arms. As the sale opened, each basket was divided among the number of hands touching it. The supply to each was meager. Thus, Bob had some of the fish-plant workers build an area alongside our house where we started a hydroponic garden. After that we were the envy of the islanders.

There were still foods that we craved, like raisins, nuts, berries, cheese and chocolate, etc. Visitors arriving in Palau would often fill their pockets and suitcases with some of the above, even lettuce. This didn't work for ice cream. I had the foresight to bring along an ice-cream maker and soon was making coconut, papaya, pineapple, mango, and a durian-fruit ice cream. We nicknamed the durian fruit, "football fruit" because of its shape. The locals would not touch it because of its foul smell. This is a spiky fruit native to Southeast Asia and some say it smells like garbage, or rotting fish, or dead cats. Inside there were pale-yellow-fleshy segments with the consistency of a pulpy custard. It tasted like a sweet onion pudding to us. Other varieties may have a different flavor.

At times there were ceremonial feasts or luas where a whole roasted pig and crocodile were laid out on a table side by side upon palm fronds or pandanus leaves. Our backyard had the only pig pit on the island and was in demand for these roasts. Early in the morning the cavity of the pig was filled with red-hot coals and then placed on palm leaves in the pit. Layers of more hot coals, with a final layer of leaves, and finally burlap were heaped on top. The pig was then left to roast about twelve hours. If we were not invited to the feast, we were always ready with our plate when the roasting was completed. This was generously given. It is said that the part of the pig or crocodile given depended on one's standing in the clan.

The fruit bat, with a wing span of about two feet, was another delicacy which the locals traditionally made into a coconut-bat soup. The preparation of this dish involves immersing live fruit bats, fur and all, into boiling water to be cooked. This produces a characteristic musky odor. The bat is then skinned and the meat picked off the bones to return to the broth. It is served with coconut milk and I am told the flavor is exquisite. I was curious one day to see inside a fish freezer across the lagoon from us. Upon entry I was horrified at the sight of dozens of furry fruit bats hanging there in their entirety so close to my head. Needless to say, I never did try this cuisine.

On weekends we would take a motor boat and find a sandy beach among the Rock Islands. These were formed by limestone or coral up rises. Most are umbrella-like shapes and famous for their surrounding blue lagoons and marine life. Here we could spend an afternoon snorkeling while being ever mindful of sharks venturing too close to the shore. Searching for shells while swimming among the colorful fish and coral was a favorite pastime. Later, I would bury our shell catch in the backyard for a month to clean out the animal inside. The secret to maintaining a nice shine to the shells was to keep them out of the sunlight. Other times we would glide the boat through the mangrove swamps, ever conscious of the crocodiles looming nearby.

Living near us was an artisan who made jewelry out of the crocodile teeth. He would take a whole tooth and dangle it inside a circle of turtle shell to make a necklace or earrings, or, he would take teeth of various sizes and space them on a chain of black coral. There were other artisans at the local jail making storyboards. These are boards often cut into the shape of an animal and then carved depicting local folk lore. These works of art were finished with a stain of local plant colors and then brought to a shine with ordinary shoe polish. One is the story of stone money.

Jewelry made from crocodile teeth, turtle shells and black coral

One day while sitting alongside the beach in Yap, a fisherman noticed a huge piece of stone resembling the moon. There were many of these stones which could reach many feet in diameter. They were flat and had a donut hole in the center. The tale goes that some of these were transported

from Yap to Palau by outrigger canoe. The trip
is about 250 miles. The more perilous the expedition, the greater the value of the stone. These
stones are so difficult to move and in Yap they dot
the islands propped against stacks of stones. They
are used primarily for huge transactions such as
marriage arrangements and land purchases. They
are generally never moved. Palauan folk tales say
they moved some stones from Yap to Palau, but I
never saw these stones in Palau. I am told there are
many. Who knows? It is just a folk tale. I can only
go by the storyboard I bought, and photos.

Another storyboard depicts a tale of fish. There
was an old women living alone in her village. Her
son traveled throughout other villages so she seldom saw him. Fishermen would pass her home each
day with their catch but never offered her any. She
was particularly fond of certain fish but was never
able to eat any. When her son came home one day,
she complained that others had plenty to eat but
she never had a fish in her pot. He went out into his
mother's yard and near the water's edge he found a
breadfruit tree. He cut off one of the branches and
immediately water rushed out from the tree, flow-
ing spasmodically to the rhythm of the waves on

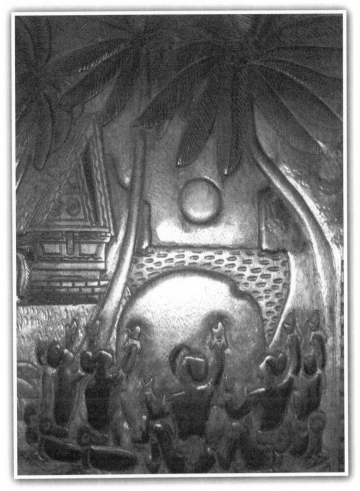

Storyboard depicting a Palauan Bai,
moon and stone money

the shore. With each surge a fish leaped out of
the tree. This tree became the envy of all. While

the fishermen had to go out to sea for fish, this woman could get all she wished by sitting under her tree. Finally, an envious old man cut the tree down. The water that had previously flowed forth intermittently now burst out in a torrent and very soon the entire island was flooded. There are many such storyboard tales, many of them rather raunchy.

Storyboard depicting the story
of the old woman and fish

The prisoners at the jail, using an electric needle also carved large turtle shells with scenes similar to those on the storyboards. These were sold to tourists. I was given one, and it was a prized possession which I packed with me to our next assignment. After a couple of years it became brittle and started to peel. Also, since it is an endangered species I was concerned about going through customs in our travels, so I eventually gave it away.

We had a Palauan/American women's group. Occasionally we would take trips on an LCU (landing craft) used in WWII to transport troops and equipment. During one such trip to a village on Babelthaup Island I decided to try chewing betelnut. This nut is chewed by both men and women as a social pastime. It stains their lips, gums and teeth a bright orange-red and puts them in a state of euphoria. Can you imagine a smiling red-mouthed Palauan with many missing teeth as a result of chewing betelnut? They chew the nut down to a fibrous residue, which is normally spit out on the streets. These women spat into an empty coca-cola can. I could not bring myself to do the same, so I would excuse myself and spit outside in private. It was like chewing a dried twig. Needless to say, I never graduated to a second betelnut.

Pictographs on the ceiling beams inside the Bai

At the Palau museum is a *Bai,* once used for a men's council and meeting house. Now it is used for any meeting or function. It is well known for its architectural beauty, with its steep-pitched palm thatch roof, its ornamental framework, and decorative pictographs on the tie beams and gables, painted in ochre, black, yellow, red and white.

There was still evidence of Japanese control after WWII. Many adults on the island spoke Japanese besides Palauan and English. Sunken, rusted Japanese and American boats and airplanes lined the lagoons where children would jump and laugh and play. Seaplane ramps were still in use, where poisonous sea snakes lurked in pairs.

Every few months a field-trip ship visited the outer islands carrying a doctor, a dentist, and a priest, and yes, cigarettes and beer. Islanders only had the use of these professionals for a day so health care was almost non-existent. The missionaries often warned the locals of their custom of burying alive their deformed children.

It was the custom that if someone borrowed something from you, he did not have to return it as his need might be greater than yours. Only if he died, the family had to return it. Also, upon death, a person's personal possessions were often buried with him.

I had two maids, and I would often give them articles of clothing. Later, I would go into the office and find a secretary wearing my clothing. This upset me, but there was nothing I could do. Under the clan system, one must always yield to one higher up when asked.

One of my maids had several children, with two of them living with relatives in Guam. She heard that they were being abused and wanted to bring them back. I set up an account for her at the local bank and then deposited part of her earnings there until she had accumulated the amount needed for her airfare to Guam. The morning of her departure, she went to the bank to withdraw funds for her ticket, only to find that her account had had been cleaned out by someone higher up in her clan. Her extended family would also charge their food purchases on her account, which she had to pay at the end of the month. There was no getting ahead for her. Palau is a matriarchal society so how could a man withdraw a woman's funds from the bank? Oh yes, he was the highest of the clan and a US Senator.

It was hard to say who was related to whom among Palauans. At the age of puberty young girls were paired with a young boy to learn the ways of life. If a child resulted in this union, it was taken away from the young couple and given to an aunt or other relative to raise. These children often didn't know who their biological parents were. It seems that it was just not important to them.

Since there were no clothing stores in Palau, I had to depend on my sister in California to send me her children's clothing, as they were just a year older than mine. At first, she sent me only the best. Later, because of the Palauan sharing system, I asked her to send all that she had. When traveling outside of Palau, I always made sure to buy many duplicates and sizes of children's clothing as I never knew when I would get another chance to purchase more. I decided that I could possibly buy clothing and other items from the Sears-Roebuck Catalog. I just happened to have one with me. I sent in an order by mail, but there was a definite problem of delivery. The company required that we have a physical address to deliver to. How could this be accomplished? We had no street addresses so I sent in a reply stating that from the airport at Babelthaup one would take the ferry to the main island, Koror. Then drive the length of the town, also known as Koror, and proceed across a very short causeway to the small island of Malakal. A mile or so down the road on the left one would find the fisheries compound where we lived. Oh yes, the speed limit is five miles per hour because of the deep potholes. This was just not an acceptable address for Sears, so the idea of ordering from them was dropped. The small post office in town didn't have an address for delivery either and wouldn't accept packages anyway. We would just have to find another use for our Sears Catalog.

We had no TV and no library on the island. When a large ship came to port we were always invited aboard where we could exchange pocket books. We also enjoyed a delicious meal, after which the Captain would open the ship's freezers and gift us with several large cuts of meat. Living on the islands, we always found one way or another to get by.

The fisheries company back in the US published their earnings from the previous year and foolishly sent pamphlets announcing this to our office staff. The workers then took it upon themselves to ask for a 25% pay raise, which the company refused. Unrest prevailed, and one day in protest the locals tried to sink some of the fishing boats tied up to our dock. Failing this, they then set the gauges in the plant so high that it could have blown up the entire plant, including our house. Luckily, Bob recognized this danger and was able to reset the gauges to ensure safety. One afternoon, we were taken out to lunch by the local senator and his wife. She was part of our women's group and a good friend. As we sat at the table, the senator warned us to be careful, as something could happen. Then, that very night at two a.m. our house was bombed.

There were hoards of people standing outside the fence at this hour of the morning, knowing that something was to happen. Two Molotov cocktails were thrown over the fence and under our mobile home. They exploded, with dishes flying off the shelves, pictures falling off the walls, and the floor buckling up about a foot. There was no electricity.

Ever since that day, my son Robert, who was the closest to where the bombs exploded, is very sensitive to noise. Later, while in Guam, with this experience still fresh in his mind, he would run and throw his arms around my legs anytime a plane flew overhead. To this day, subconsciously, he has never really gotten over that sensitivity. The police finally arrived and escorted us up into the hills, where we hid out at a friend's house until a plane arrived two days later to get us out of Palau. The children and I were taken to a luxury hotel in Guam until Bob was able to join us some days later. Within a week the company sent us to the Phillipines for a month of rest and recuperation. After that, the company bribed us to return to Palau, which we did. Shortly afterwards my dad and his new wife arrived on the island for a two-month visit. Since the elderly in Palau were treated with great respect, we had no trouble during their visit.

Bob and I took this opportunity of built in babysitters to take a quick trip together to Guam. On the day of our return, my dad, along with the company driver and the children, took the ferry from Koror to the airport on the island of Bablethuap. This ferry consisted of a wooden platform carrying only a few cars and was pulled across the straight by ropes. A storm was forming and the waters in the straight were rising and churning. On the return from the airport the waters were so high that the driver walked in front of the car with a stick to determine how high the water was. It was hard to see where the road was. We were forced to turn back to the terminal, which was a bombed out cement structure left over from WWII. It was a short distance from the airport. Our Seabee (US Navy Construction Crew) friends had a camp nearby and came to our rescue. My dad had not thought to bring along a change of clothing for the children and Karina was still in diapers. The Seabees made a fire which they used to dry her one diaper when needed. Then they asked at some of the nearby shacks to borrow sheets and such to bed down the children in the car. Karina slept comfortably on the ledge of the back window. The next morning we were able to continue our trip back to Malakal, where my step-mother was waiting. She hadn't been concerned at all and thought it very reminiscent of Canadian storms. It wasn't too long after that incident that my dad and his wife returned to Canada.

Shortly after their departure, we began to feel uneasy again. Bob was constantly warned to be careful, as something could happen to his wife and children. One day Bob gave me some money and a note with instructions to go down to the ferry and find an obvious tourist. Giving them the money and note, I asked them to take a taxi to the company lawyer in Guam. We were soon off the island and it was sad to say,

Ak Morolung ... I am leaving; *Mechikung* ... *Goodbye*

Kuwait ..... mid 1975 to mid 1976

We only spent six months in Guam before Bob was offered a job by the Kuwait Government to enhance their shrimp industry. When I told my two young children that we would be moving again, they ran to their bedroom. Several minutes later they came out, each with their short arms wrapped around a brown shopping bag full of toys and clothing, and announced, "OK Mom, we're ready. Let's go."

We flew from Guam over the Philippines, the South China Sea, the Bay of Bengal, the South of

India, the Arabian Sea, and then to the mouth of the Persian Gulf. By this time we were in a terrible sand storm that made visibility difficult even at our altitude. I was very frightened while clinging to my children. We set down at Abu Dhabi in the Persian Gulf to wait for climate conditions to clear. While passing through immigration, I was asked to surrender our passports. I was reluctant to do this as I was traveling alone with my young children clutching each firmly. I waited for the Air-France Captain to deboard and related my concern. He assured me this was the custom, and I had no choice. Passports would be returned upon our departure. I was still uneasy. The next line was to pick up our taxi, hotel and meal vouchers. I was still concerned, so I asked a Filipino man I had spoken to on board the flight if we could link our vouchers together. He was so understanding, polite and agreeable. I held onto that voucher tightly and my new friend could not make a move without me. I seemed to be the only woman at the hotel. The dining room was filled with men only, clothed in their long white garb. I would not enter this world so asked permission to take my meals in the lobby, with my Filipino man tagging along as escort, of course. The next morning we continued our flight to Kuwait and my new-found friend stayed with me until Bob greeted us, extending a handshake and a grateful "thank you" to our friend.

Kuwait lies along the Persian Gulf with a land mass of 17,820 square kilometers and a fairly flat terrain. It lies at the northwest corner of the Persian Gulf and is located between Saudi Arabia to the south and southwest, and Iraq to the north.

We settled into a very large, modern-furnished apartment. Normally Kuwait kitchens do not have cupboards, or any appliances, just the bare walls. We were lucky, as we had all that, I suppose because it was a government apartment. Our kitchen was situated down a long hallway near the front door away from the rest of the apartment. We had a typical British washing machine that held a maximum of one sheet. It contained a separate compartment with a spin cycle, but after that I had to hang the clothes around the apartment.

Temperatures in Kuwait averaged 110 degrees from May through September. It was too hot to go outside during the daytime, so we waited until Bob came home around 8 p.m. Even when venturing outside at that hour, we found that a blast of warm air in our face was unbearable. We tried venturing down to the swimming pool a couple of times during the day but the high brick wall surrounding the compound kept that heat contained. I never saw the pool being cleaned, so I was positive it was not safe.

We could not stand the conditions of this home life, and I contemplated moving back to Vancouver for the duration of Bob's one-year contract with the Kuwait Fisheries. About that time an American friend suggested that maybe we would be more comfortable moving 25 miles south of the city to the Kuwait oil town of Fahaheel. There was a British social club there called the Gazelle Club situated right on the Persian Gulf. We rented a motel room just outside the walls of the club. It had one large room with a tall bookcase division which became the children's bedroom. At first we rented a couple of cots for the children from the motel but learned that if we had bunk beds made, there would be no room charge for them. The room boy even changed the bunk-bed sheets every day with no charge. The bathroom was huge. The water was so rusty that I had to wrap a towel around the faucet to eliminate some of this discoloration. The same procedure was used to filter the water while hosing it to our tiny washing machine which was placed atop the toilet seat. Again, we had no dryer. At first we took our meals at the Gazelle Club, but soon tired of that. Bob had some supply cupboards built in the bathroom and the main room. We bought a small kettle and some dishes. An electric fry pan was our main cooking utensil. With these limited supplies we could make delicious one-pan meals, the main one being the huge prawns that Bob brought home from the fish plant. We ate shrimp like hamburger.

The Gazelle Club offered many activities and entertainment. There was a playground for the children. We had a clean swimming pool along the Persian Gulf, and the Gulf itself to swim in among the hundreds of tiny fish. There were horses to feed, a bowling alley, movies a few times a week and social times. The restaurant was good, and the children ate there free.

Children start school the quarter they turn four in the British Schools. So in January 1976, Robert went off to school in his uniform of blue short pants and a white shirt. The oil companies supplied a bus for the children. Since they had only a few children, others were invited to use the system as well. One parent would always accompany them on the bus to school, and then the mothers would take turns picking up the children after school. About the same time, I heard of a Scottish lady running a pre-school out of her home, so I enrolled my daughter there. Karina was fascinated by her lavish home and often came home saying, "Mrs. Martin has a beautiful bathroom; we don't have a beautiful bathroom."

Many of the 140 fishing boats in Kuwait were inoperable, so that was Bob's first job - to get the fleet back to work in the Persian Gulf. Kuwait was one of the world's largest shrimp exporters. By custom only men worked at the fish processing plant, as women were not to be seen. Bob arranged for them to be picked up inconspicuously from their homes each morning and transported to the plant. He walled in an area for them to work. Noticing that they would squat on the floor to sort the shrimp, he ordered tables built so they could stand. After that they would squat on the tables to work. At least he tried, and now some of the women in Kuwait were at work.

When our one-year contract was up in Kuwait Bob took a job in Saudi Arabia. The children and I went on home-leave to Newport, Oregon, and prepared to return to the Middle East. This did not happen, as Bob joined us in Oregon within two months.

Ma'a salama!.... *goodbye*

Kids say ..... Fish is Delish on a Dish

*B*ob purchased a boat, the Mitoi, a mid-water trawler. He said this was his semi-retirement, what he had always dreamt about. We bought a lovely home overlooking the Newport, Oregon, bayfront and from there I could watch the fishing boats coming and going. I did not work while in Newport, as I had all I could handle with the children and managing our fishing business.

I joined the Fishermen's Wives' group which was basically formed to promote the fishing industry.

Bob was only licensed to fish for halibut, sole, hake, bass and perch. Crab and other species would invariably be tangled in his net. He did not like to throw back undersized fish as they would not survive anyway due to larger predators. Others argued that it was food for these predators. Anyway he refused to throw them back in the ocean. For awhile Bob had a group who would stand outside on the sidewalk in front of the fish plant and just give these fish away. Later, he arranged to take the fish to a nearby park where local seniors could come and take home whatever they could filet. Bob would often come home from a trip with a few live crab under his sweat shirt. We had many welcome feasts from that.

For two years in succession, through the Fishermen's Wives, I received a grant from the National Marine Fisheries for $75,000. With this I hired Vi Shepard, Home Economist and Seafood Consultant, to go into the schools. We took the extra fish to the classrooms and taught the students how to filet and cook the fish. Before fileting them we would make *Gyotaku,* Japanese Fish Prints. First, a thin coat of ink is brushed on the fish. Then an absorbent paper is carefully placed over the inked fish and the entire fish is gently rubbed with the fingers to transfer the ink to the paper. The print is then carefully removed and the eyes are painted on by hand. Then it was time to filet and cook the fish. After consuming this most nutritious dish, the children would often ask for the recipe to take home to their mothers. Thus we set out to collect recipes tried and true in the classroom to publish a cookbook. There was a contest for the title of the book, **Kids say .... Fish is Delish on a Dish**, and students did the art work. Eventually some of the recipes were introduced into the school lunch menu.

Gyotaku

The fishing industry had many hardships. We lost the Mitoi at the mouth of the Columbia River. Bob had pulled up a particularly large catch and the pendulum motion of the net caused the boat to overturn. The crew of three were able to climb up onto the hull of the boat and there they stayed for hours while trying to catch the attention of other boats. Bob asked one of the crew to dive under to find the tracking transmitter box as it had not dislodged from its case and popped to the surface. The purpose of this box was to send out a signal of distress. Finally, the fisherman found his courage to dive. Unfortunately, he hit his hand after retrieving the box and it slipped away to the bottom of the sea. Just before dusk a Coast Guard boat happened by and put them in tow, but the weight of the catch in the net just pulled the boat down to the bottom of the sea. All the crew were thankfully saved. Two days later, the box did surface and an overhead airplane picked up the signal.

Bob's next boat was the Pioneer, another midwater trawler which he fished for a few years. During that time he lost one crewman overboard, a tragic loss. By this time the allowance of fish to be caught was greatly reduced, and it was impossible to bring in enough fish to pay for the cost of paying the crew. New nets were $10,000 each, and other general maintenance was costly. A net could easily snag on the bottom of the ocean and be lost the first trip. It was 1983 by then and the interest rates on boat mortgages had gone up to about eighteen percent from the original rate on a million dollar boat of about ten percent. That year we lost our home, which was mortgaged for the boat, as well as other property. As a last attempt to salvage our livelihood, Bob went to Alaska and fished in the Bering Sea near the Russian border. Due to the previous problems in Oregon, it was too late to sign on for the season with a large fish company. He could only fish for bait to be off loaded at sea to other fishing boats.

It was a poor season and finally he was forced to give up the Pioneer. We heard that it was later auctioned off for $25,000, an amount we did not have to get Bob's dream back. Many fishermen down the length of the Pacific Coast who did not have their boats paid off that year lost their homes and boats as well….. their livelihood.

Within two weeks after this disastrous end to our fisheries adventure Bob was off to the Marshall Islands.

My son, daughter and I have visited Monterey, California a couple of times in the past few years and to our surprise saw the Pioneer anchored there in great disrepair. Thankfully, it has now been refurbished and ready to set out on a fishing trip.

Marshall Islands Atoll, the Crest of a Dying Volcano

I n 1788 Capt. Thomas Gilbert and Capt. John Marshall were chartered by the East India Company to ship tea from China to England. En-route they passed by two island-atoll groups, naming one the Gilbert Islands and the other the Marshall Islands. An atoll is a crest formed on layers of dead coral far above a volcano. The coral from the volcano deep under water rises to the surface to replenish itself.

We arrived in the Marshall Islands in April 1984 as Bob had been rehired by FAO to help revive the fishing industry in the islands. We were given housing on a family compound very near the southern end of the atoll. It was a very modest house with a large kitchen-dining-living room area, three bedrooms and two bathrooms (showers only) one of which was piled high with boxes as our only storage area. On a kitchen outside wall, where one would normally find baseboards, was a hole so the water could flow back outside if the lagoon waters should rise. Luckily we did not experience any tidal waves during our two years living in the Marshalls and our house remained dry. As an added insurance, our house was situated on the widest part of the atoll. I had been told that during such unfortunate flooding times a lot of the island population congregated on our property. In many areas along the lagoon one could throw a football from the main road into the Pacific Ocean, or, in the opposite direction, into the lagoon. Household water was a sad joke, or should I say almost nonexistent. Water was collected on the airport runway and piped approximately 30 miles around the horseshoe atoll to our little abode situated almost to the end of the pipeline. Age and misuse managed to puncture many holes in the pipes along the way, so our water supply was almost a trickle. In our daily life dishes had to be stacked in the sink, clothes washing was minimal, swimming in the lagoon became a necessity for hygiene, and my 12-year-old son had to lug buckets of water from the lagoon to flush the toilet. During the dry season water was turned on only every other day between five and seven p.m. Life revolved around this major event. Since there was more of a gush around five p.m., our first priority was to give the toilet a much needed flush. Next in importance was to quickly wash the dishes before filling the washing machine for at least one load. Then we filled as many pots and buckets with fresh water as time allowed, leaving the final few minutes for a shower and hair wash. We had to take turns with this latter necessity before the last trickle gave out, leaving some of us to wait another two days. Luckily the lagoon was not far from our back door. We did have a cement water-catchment tank under a large tree along one side of the house. The water flowed off the roof into the gutters and piped into the tank; however, there was no pump to further carry the water into the house. It took a few months before Bob could acquire the much needed parts, and I can still visualize him with my son, Robert, out in the blazing heat trying to hook up the system to the house. What a blessing to finally have our own water, even though it was dependent on future rainfalls. Since the catchment tank was noticeably polluted by falling leaves, geckos, and other undesirable life forms, we learned, as in our previous experiences in Indonesia and the Caroline Islands of Palau, to boil our water at least twenty minutes to make it potable - just one more exercise in our struggle of existence.

Karina found many new friends. Some were the geckos (subtropical lizards) which crawled the walls and ceilings and would hang around inside the ceiling lighting fixtures in the house. They ate bugs and spiders. Karina treated them as pets and named each one. There was a George, a Fred and a Charlie to name a few. She was also delighted with the baby ducks, chickens and pigs. They scavenged the beaches when let loose, and wandered into our yard.

Our little yellow house had a white picket fence surrounding it with a huge flame tree in the front yard and another in the back, on the lagoon side. These umbrella-like trees were a burst of color with flaming, red blossoms. They were so pictur-esque, especially when I would find my 12-year-old daughter, Karina, hanging in the branches along with some of the local children.

There was another small house between ours and the lagoon, where a Marshallese family lived with their seven sons. From my kitchen window, I could look into their large yard where Robert would join all the boys in a game of baseball. They used an old two-by-four as a bat. I loved looking out at the lagoon, but was annoyed one day to see these same boys using an equally large stick to poke at a turtle. This particular turtle when caught was left outside lying on its back for a few days, thus there was the opportunity for the boys to torture it. The turtles in the lagoon could easily reach three to four feet in length, and the locals would catch them for the meat content. Turtles are endangered, so in order not to be caught the Marshallese would often times just throw the empty shell back into the lagoon. What a waste and a shame to see them on the sandy bottom of the lagoon through the shiny blue waters.

In this same neighbor's yard was a small shack where a few Marshallese women would congregate.

I asked to join them one day and found them all squatted on the floor making head leis for a festival the next day. It looked so easy as they formed perfectly symmetrical floral *heis*. Much to the amusement of the women, I just could not form the same perfect arrangements. My *heis* were useless, so in order not to embarrass myself further, I decided to leave, thus not taking up more of their time. They still had a huge task ahead of them. It was very common to see these adornments around the islands on a daily basis, and it made me feel very special whenever I was presented with one. For Mother's Day my daughter, Karina, was presented with a beautiful *heis* as a symbol of future motherhood.

On one side of our property was a chain-link fence separating us from another neighbor. Although I could not converse with the old grandmother, I liked to watch her as she squatted while washing the family's clothing in a large metal tub. I felt somewhat guilty as I had my own washing machine inside. She didn't seem to mind, as she always had a huge toothless grin for me. She always placed her washtub right up against the fence, so I assumed that she liked to watch us as well. It gave me the sense of how proud the Marshallese women are, or was it inferiority, or curiousness, or just friendliness. I tend to believe the latter.

Since the neighbors had such lush foliage in their yards, we decided that we would create something equally interesting. Bob brought in a truck load of copra-coke (ground up coconut shells) to mix in with our sandy soil. Again, we were the amusement of the neighborhood as we planted our vegetable seeds. In the coming months we were watched closely. I was embarrassed again when nothing would grow so close to the sea water. In spite of all this, we were living in paradise. A popular hit song that I heard daily on the radio was, "Islands in the Sun," and I felt so lucky to be living in this magical paradise.

I recall the first days when we took Robert and Karina to the lagoon and watched their excitement. They had always gone swimming in a pool with the edge of the pool for their security. Here they were cast upon this world of a vast blue lagoon of clear and warm water. Our intention was to teach them to snorkel, but the vastness was initially too overwhelming for them. Because both were excellent swimmers, they finally took off, but stayed together like two porpoises, frequently surfacing to exclaim at the clearness of the water, the abundance

and variety of fish, and, of course, the unforget-
table colors of the fish, coral, and sea shells. In my
mind I will always visualize the pair swimming in
such proximity and sharing every detail.

More foods and plants in the South Pacific:

The **Papaya** is found on most large
Marshall islands, but seldom in any abundance. There are about 20 different varieties
of papaya. The tree can grow to the height
of 20 feet. It is cultivated from a seed and
three types of plants may grow from the
seed. One plant may only contain the male
flower and another may contain only the
female flower. Another seed may contain
both the male and female parts on the same
plant. The new plant will develop and bear
fruit before the end of the first year, and then
will continue to produce from three to five
years more. After this time the plants are cut
down. There is no special season, as fruiting
is continuous during the life of the plant.
The fruit is melon like in character. Its
shape is oblong to globular and ranges from

three to as much as 20" in length. Its flesh is about one inch thick, ranging from deep yellow to salmon in color. In the central cavity there are numerous pea-size seeds. The ripe fruit has a yellow outer skin. It is very flavorful and slightly sweet, somewhat like a cantaloupe. Ripe papaya can be eaten fresh sprinkled with salt and lemon juice, or with sugar. When it is green, it may be cooked and eaten as a vegetable. In the Marshalls the people commonly wrap tough chicken or other meat with the papaya leaves and leave it over night as this has a tenderizing effect. The silky substance which is found in the leaf parts as well as in the rind of the green fruit, contains papain. Green papaya cut up in stews will tenderize the meat. The bark of the papaya tree is used to make rope, and the roots yield a juice used as a nerve tonic.

The **Breadfruit** tree grows to a height of 40 to 60 feet and is the second most important crop of the Marshall Islands. There are many varieties of the breadfruit and each has its own characteristic leaf and shape. Its branches are frail and easily broken and its timber is soft. The leathery leaves grow to enormous dimensions and they range from almost unlobed to having seven to nine deep, narrow lobes with deep veins going from the midrib to the leaf margin. The fruit generally ripens from May to July; however fruit may be seen as late as December. It is usually gathered before it reaches full ripeness when the flesh is firm, white, mealy and rich in starch. It is best baked whole, boiled, steamed or roasted in an open pit. It is called breadfruit because it tastes like plain bread. The fruit is melon shaped and is about eight inches in diameter. It has a rough-surface outer skin which is yellowish-green in color. When it is fully ripe it has a sweet taste and goes bad very quickly. Most varieties are seedless, but two or three varieties have a seed which is edible and resembles a chestnut both in size and shape. These are boiled and then roasted in an open oven called an *um*. The Marshallese people of the outer islands have a method of preserving the breadfruit so that it can be used as a food all year. In this process the fruit is cut in half, both the skin and the core are removed, and then it is marinated over night in sea water. After being taken from the sea, it is left outside to soften for about a day. It is then put into a pit which is lined with leaves and covered with dried breadfruit leaves. It is kneaded daily while it ferments. This will keep for as long as six months. The preserved breadfruit becomes sticky and at this stage it is mixed with coconut milk and coconut syrup, then wrapped in fresh breadfruit leaves and baked in the oven or roasted in an open fire. The sticky paste may also be boiled in water and then dropped into boiling coconut milk to produce a dumpling.

Other uses of the breadfruit:

The trunk produces timber for huts, houses, and canoe hulls. When the sticky, white, milky latex hardens, it makes a calking to waterproof canoes. The leaves serve as roofing materials and wrappings for food. The dried spikes of the male flower are used for tinder wood. The Marshallese kindle fires of these spikes to repel mosquitos.

There are about 100 different varieties of the **Pandanus**. The long slender leaves are useful for making many artifacts. The dried fallen leaves are gathered, trimmed of the spiny edges, rolled into a coil and thus stored. When these coils are needed, they are re-rolled in the opposite direction, causing them to straighten and remain flat. The spiny mid-rib is then removed and the leaf is easily split into the desired width using the thumbnail. It may then be woven, or plaited into baskets, mats, fans, thatch, etc. These are all popular items among tourists and islanders alike. The pandanus fruit matures in late October to January. In outward appearance the mature fruit, which is a dark green resembles the pine-apple. When separated from the whole fruit, individual segments are found to be white in color at the center and orange at the inner end. The ripe fruit may be boiled like a vegetable or chewed raw. When the pandanus is baked in an earth oven, it is possible to scrape off the starchy pulp and dry it to a flour consistency. This can be made into a paste. In this form it has storage qualities. Many children enjoy

chewing the inner end of a pandanus segment (Marshallese candy.) As they chew, they
rotate the segment and extract the sweet tast-
ing starchy pulp from the tough and stringy
fibers. When the ripe fruit falls and the segments separate and dry the fibrous inner end
may be used as a paint brush.

We couldn't fully settle in until our much-awaited
container shipment with our much-needed household
goods and our brand-new Boston Whaler motor boat
arrived. There was great excitement as the neighborhood came out to gawk while we unpacked such oddi-
ties as a washer and dryer. There was no lack of help as
we dragged the boat from the container to the lagoon
with the youngest of children already seated inside
awaiting a much-anticipated ride on the lagoon. They
were not disappointed as the boat left the shore well
laden down with smiling faces.

We were excited to start our weekend adventures
with our new boat, scouting out the many islands
along the atoll. Sand and water moved around the
ocean shaping these island worlds where coral reefs
sparkle under the sunlit water. Each island became
a special place for us. Most were uninhabited or

with maybe one extended family living there. As a family, we explored the sandy beaches in search of shells and traipsed the narrow, coconut-palmed islands. Snorkeling for shells became a favorite and time-consuming adventure. We obviously were inept at climbing the coconut trees, and those fallen fruit were for cooking, not for drinking, even if we could master the art of opening them. We had a lot to learn.

It was not too long before we chose Calalin as our favorite island. It was situated almost at the end of the atoll chain where one extended family lived. A huge pandanus tree partially shaded the sandy beach, so we tied our four hammocks around it for sleeping. This did not make for a comfortable night as it curved the spine, which I could not endure for an entire night's sleep. Thus I took to sleeping on the soft sand, becoming another obstacle for the numerous hermit crabs to crawl around and over. It was still better than the hammock. I recall that during one rain storm an elder approached our hammock tree late at night and gestured that we sleep underneath a shelter that served as their cooking shack.

Our only spoken communication with our new friends was *"iakwe* (yakweh,)" their island greeting which loosely translated means, "you are the rainbow; greetings, and love."

Nevertheless, we soon learned their needs and wants and began arriving with gifts of coffee, flour, sugar, cigarettes, and beer. After all, we were guests on their island. On a typical day, as we approached Calalin, we were welcomed by the waving coconut trees and could catch a glimpse of a youngster or two scampering high in the palms. Then as our boat glided toward shore, they would wade out with a fresh coconut for each of us to quench our thirst. At the same time, the women busied themselves weaving pandanus baskets and plates which were also presented for our use. We normally brought our own food, but it wasn't long before we were sitting around in groups sharing what we each had to offer. There was one food made of taro that I definitely avoided as I sat one day watching an elderly woman prepare it. She was squatted on the sand kneading the taro which had been fermented and kneaded each day for a period of time. On this particular day she was about to wrap her prized creation in banana leaves. I was shocked to see yellowish worm-like creatures crawling in the dough. When I pointed this out, she just smiled and laughed and poked at these disgusting creatures. I'll always remember this gesture as she grinned her widest smile, thus showing her equally disgusting betelnut-stained teeth. Other than this finding, I found the island village to be extremely clean.

Early each morning I watched as the women swept the entire area including the sandy beach. I was always fascinated that after the sweeping, the only tracks on the sand were from the webbed feet of wild chickens.

The Calalin islanders carefully watched each weekend as we snorkeled and combed the beaches for shells. You can imagine my excitement when one day they came to me in procession offering me lovely shells they had gleaned from the reefs while fishing. Shells found in the ocean or under the rocks on the reefs have a natural shine to them and the object is to clean out the creatures from within without losing this shine. So back on Majuro Island, I designated a small patch in our back yard, as I had done in Palau, to clean out the shells. For the next month ants would eat the creatures inside leaving nothing but a slimy, smelly, but shiny shell.

Occasionally we would go out on the lagoon for a day with our Marshallese friends. There was no dock at our back-yard lagoon so the ladies would swim out to the boats with the skirts of their dresses billowing atop of the water. The women never wear shorts or bathing suits but neat floral-cotton dresses as dictated by custom. Upon returning home in the late afternoons, they repeated the same ritual as the ladies jumped off the boat and swam for shore. Of course we did the same but felt more comfortable wearing bathing attire.

My thirteen-year-old son, Robert, took a job with the local grocery store as a stock boy. One of his jobs was to travel by motor boat to the island of Mili some 70 miles away, taking them food and other supplies. I wasn't too happy about this venture as the seas could get very treacherous and the small copra boat was not properly maintained or equipped with life jackets. As a typical boy he never told me stories about things he thought I was better off not knowing. All I knew was that each trip he came home safely.

Scattered throughout the Pacific are field-trip ships which make their rounds to the outer islands about every three or four months. Even though they are called "ships," they are really just mid-sized motorized boats. They usually take along a doctor and a dentist as well as the very basic food supplies of rice, flour, sugar, canned tuna, sodas, and coffee. Somewhere in there was what the natives deemed necessary, cigarettes and beer. In exchange they would bring back Copra, the dried coconut meat from which coconut oil is made. They often took passengers, but we had no desire or time to take such a trip.

I had my own experience on an outer island. Some American friends, Dado and Peggy, had started an oyster farm on the island of Arno, east of Majuro. I was invited to visit and took the opportunity to go along when a group of FAO officials went to visit. My intention was to only stay the weekend and take a plane back to Majuro from another island across the lagoon from Arno. When it came time to leave, however, I was told that the scheduled plane would not arrive as the Islanders had not felt like cleaning the debris from a recent storm on the small airport runway across the lagoon. So, I settled in to enjoy my adventure on Arno with my host friends. I was housed in a pandanus-leaf shack with a sand floor and a thatched roof. It was right beside the lagoon and the warm breezes would flow through each night, thus blowing off part of the roof bit by bit. Luckily I did not get rained on, but in this anticipation a crew of natives arrived one morning dragging large palm fronds along the sandy path and did an extensive roof repair for me as I looked on curiously and gratefully.

Because we were so near the equator, the sun set around 6 p.m. It could get quite eerie in the dark evenings with the wind blowing, palm fronds cracking and falling, and the thud of coconuts crashing to the ground. After our evening meal in the dining shack I would have to walk the winding path alone with just a dim lantern to guide me to my shack. It could be pitch black unless the moon was showing its face. Once inside there was nothing to do but scurry into my cot, from which I could hear waves washing up on the shore. I had noticed water marks inside on the sandy floor, so I would often get up in the middle of the night and wander outside to see if l was still on shore. The bathroom facilities were the lagoon just outside my door, or the ocean not too far off on the other side of the atoll.

The island of Arno was very organized. Pathways had been cleared and covered with clean, white-coral sand brought up in buckets from the beach. White stones lined these paths and many varieties of small tropical plants and huge pandanus trees waved freely alongside to the lull of constant tropical breezes. Near the docking area was a small cook shack and a dining/meeting shack, all made of pandanus leaves. Scattered around the area were various other living quarters, all fashioned in the same style. These were mostly for the native workers on the oyster farm.

Every morning these workers would start the day off in their small fishing canoes, always returning with a spear full of fish. Next they would squat at the edge of the lagoon to clean and filet their catch. This was the main meal of the day. The rest of us would go into the forest and snip off the tips of certain ferns which were scrumptious as a salad. Dado, my host, had felled a row of palm trees which were lined up, lying half on the sand and half in the lagoon. From these he would cut out, as needed, the hearts of palm. This is the part just at the top of the trunk before the leaves branch out. These hearts were preserved by pickling and then placed in a large jar which sat on a shelf in the cook shack for nibbling or for adding to salads. It seems sad to think that a healthy tree had to be cut down for just a few hearts of palm, but in this case they were felled to make a clearance for an airport runway on Arno. Other basic staples such as rice, flour, sugar, oil, tea and coffee were shipped in from Majuro.

One day I couldn't resist swimming a short distance into the lagoon to inspect the oyster nets. They were hanging vertically down from the buoyed, strung together, coconut shells. With my snorkeling gear I could dive under the clear-blue water to see the tiny oysters securely attached to the netting. Unfortunately the oysters were not large enough yet for our consumption; besides they were intended for market.

Ten days later Bob, Robert and Karina arrived in a small fishing boat to fetch me. The seas were choppy, and I was very uneasy having to sail back in these conditions. There were no life jackets on board, as was typical for my husband; thus I was extremely annoyed not only because the crossing was treacherous but also because this was a lesson he was teaching our children.

There was a time when we were without our own boat, but there was a huge Catamaran tied up in the Majuro lagoon which could easily accommodate 30 people. The story went that a Canadian nurse had it built in Vancouver, Canada, hired a crew, and set out to sail the Pacific. They encountered horrible storms crossing the Pacific, lost the main mast and drifted ashore into the Majuro lagoon. Upon arrival in the Marshall Islands, this very scared lady left the boat, never to return. One of our fellow American friends took it upon himself, with the help of others, to repair and maintain the boat. He then took groups of us out on the lagoon each weekend. Even without the main mast, if we stayed within the confines of the ten-mile-wide and thirty-mile-long lagoon, we would be safe enough. As we approached our chosen island, Karina was always the first to jump off and swim to shore. Most of us just swam around and near the boat. The lagoon was always calm and clear when we set out in the mornings but could be very stormy upon our late afternoon return. I wasn't a very happy sailor then. The Canadian lady returned to Vancouver and resumed her job at the hospital until she had acquired enough money to hire a couple to return to Majuro to refit the boat with the idea of sailing it back to Canada for her. The retrofit took several months during which we continued our weekend sailings. Finally the boat was ready to depart and the idea was to sail northwest to Japan in order to catch the currents back to Vancouver. Just outside of the Majuro Lagoon, however, they realized that this boat was never intended for the open seas and they immediately returned to Majuro. The boat was abandoned once more, giving our group use of it again.

Our Boston Whaler, which we had brought from California in our shipment, turned out to be a mistake. It would slam down hard when the lagoon waters churned up. It was back wrenching. Luckily we were able to sell it to the resident American doctor. Next Bob set out to build his own small catamaran from plans FAO had developed. They already had a couple of these boats working in the Pacific. My son was delighted to help his dad build the boat in our backyard, then paint it an aquamarine with bright yellow trimmings and matching sails. I didn't go out on the initial sail which took them to the end of the lagoon to the channel leading to the ocean. He took along a few local fishermen with their young children. I went along a few days later when several Marshallese boats were to sail along the lagoon together to a picnic spot. We were lagging behind the others as the weather was picking up and I encouraged Bob to turn back. He wasn't too familiar with sailing yet and made a sharp turn upon which the boat capsized. I was trapped under a sail, struggling to get up, but the sail would repeatedly push me underwater. I could hear my son yelling, "Mom, dive down," which I finally did and found my way out from under the sail. Luckily we weren't too far from shore, but still farther that I felt comfortable with. Karina and I each grabbed a plastic water bottle which had popped up, and with these we slowly paddled to shore. We sat exhausted at the edge of the lagoon watching Bob and Robert paddling and pushing the boat towards us. All I could think of was that I was so thankful this hadn't happened when there were small children aboard at the mouth of the channel. We sat for hours on this small deserted island scanning the horizon. I didn't cherish spending the night there with no food, drink, warmth or shelter. Just before dusk we spotted a boat sailing by in the distance. They finally noticed us as we yelled, waved and jumped. They came to our rescue. The children and I clambered aboard the larger boat. Bob swam, clinging on to his dream boat, while being towed behind us.

Several Peace Corps volunteers lived and worked on the islands. They lived in whatever local housing was given them. This meant sharing a room with a Marshallese family and eating a bowl of rice topped with a bit of US canned fish as their main meal. Most homes did not have refrigeration and the food was often left without covering it or covered with flies. This is what they often came home to. We had befriended an American volunteer, Dorothy, who supposedly because of her advanced age was given a tiny shack of her own. She lived in the midst of a large extended-family compound which I loved to walk through. The neatly swept paths were in a forest of pandanus and coconut trees, the latter often laden with bunches of coconuts. Most of the living was done outdoors so the grounds outside their wooden or tin shacks were strewn with large metal pots for cooking or washing, a fire pit, maybe a pigpen, a few chickens running wild, any kind of a make-shift structure that could serve as a table or shelf, and a chair or two for the elders. The women were more comfortable squatting for whatever chore they were attending to. They also squatted to eat meals. There were various large and small appliances or sinks lying around, all of which they found a use for. Peeking out from under a large banana tree was a fuselage probably dragged up from the lagoon after WWII. I am sure it had a use as well other than being decorative or a place for the kids to play. It was touching to see the small white crosses alongside some homes, this being the custom to keep loved ones near.

Each evening starting about the first of December, we delighted at the chants echoing throughout our island atoll. This was in preparation for Christmas Day church services. On many islands groups of maybe twenty to forty would gather to practice singing and dancing. These are called "Jepta Dancers". By day the ladies would busy themselves making muumuus and matching shirts for the men. A day or so before Christmas Day the outer islanders would arrive in their canoes to participate in this charming custom.

Majuro Island would prepare for this ritual at one church at either end of the atoll and one in the middle. After an early Christmas-morning service the congregation would clear the middle of the church and then stand along the inside perimeter with the children seated cross-legged at their feet. We as foreigners were sought out and given the honor to sit in the choir chairs. The first group of dancers congregated outside the church and then would sing and shimmy and dance their way inside. Each performance lasted about half an hour during which they would throw candies at the children before dancing out. The next group would immediately make their way inside as the first group continued to the next church. As stated earlier, we lived at the end of the Island Atoll so we attended the third and last church service. These performances lasted all Christmas Day and into the night until the last group was done at about three a.m. This Christmas-Day custom could last 17 hours. Children were never on the streets that day. There was no gift opening for them and no traditional Christmas dinner as we know it. Their gifts were the candies, and they were delighted.

The Marshallese knew that we were accustomed to a Christmas dinner so around meal times they would offer us plates of food and sometimes gifts. This was a magical time for me even though I had to sneak out for periods of time to get a meal on the table for my own family, who were not so enchanted by the ritual and only stayed for part of the time.

Between Christmas and New Year's Day, groups of Jepta Dancers would visit the courtyards of some of the well-known Marshallese families to perform for them. I had noted that during that week the aroma of fresh baking wafted through the air. This was strange as the ladies of the Marshalls did not normally bake. I soon learned, however, that after each performance it was the custom to offer refreshments to the dancers. When they arrived in our courtyard on New Year's Eve, I was equally prepared and afterwards came out with some of my Canadian fruitcake and cookies. To my surprise, about an hour later, some of the women came to our door with offerings of Marshallese basketry. New Year's Eve was not over yet. At midnight sharp, the neighborhood children were out singing "We wish you a Merry

Christmas." Some of Karina's friends arrived, asking if she could go out with them door to door singing and asking for candies. I was a little nervous about this since it was midnight; but nevertheless, we knew the families and off she went. By this time the entire neighborhood knew that I made cookies. Even after the holiday season I continued to get a few knocks on my door each day with the kids bearing gifts of sea shells which I rewarded with cookies.

New Year's Day our neighbors invited us to a picnic. Upon arrival, we found the women stripping palm branches from which they would make primitive baskets to be used as plates and bowls for the food. The children were running among the tall waving coconut trees playing tag or ball, or just amusing themselves as children do. The men were standing around in groups attending the *um* (an underground oven) in which a large pig was roasting along with various other foods. Others had set up boards to use as a serving table covered with palm fronds. I could only watch, and smile and say "*yakwe.*" Another Marshallese year of fun and laughter had begun.

Marshallese woman weaving baskets

Fish feed on the coral, and humans feed on this warm-water fish which could cause ciguatera poisoning. When we first arrived on the Marshalls, we became aware of a large physical therapy facility where many people were being treated for crippled or missing limbs. We were told these afflictions were from arthritis, but how could this be? How could there be so much arthritic suffering on such a small atoll? A couple of years later, towards the end of our stay in the Marshalls, a preliminary study was revealed stating that arthritis may not be the cause, but rather poisoning caused by the consumption of fish that fed on the coral reefs. We now began to understand why the Marshallese fed their fish catch to the dogs first. There were packs of mangy dogs roaming Majuro. I suppose as a result of being fed fish from the reefs. These dogs were definitely not pets. The Marshallese did not understand that the toxicity of coral poisoning is accumulative, so only after many years of consumption was the harm obvious.

Robert and Karina were in the sixth grade when we arrived in Majuro. There were local schools, but the only one acceptable to us was a co-op from the first to eighth grade run by the parents. The teachers were hired mainly from the U.S. with a sprinkling of other foreigners. They were given local housing, which was no more than a shack, and a salary of about US200.00 dollars per month. Obviously, the attraction was for the experience of living in the South Seas. I volunteered at the school in various capacities. There were no school buildings, only some abandoned shacks by the ocean side of the atoll. Several months after we arrived, a Hawaiian department store chain was setting up in Majuro with all their supplies and goods arriving in wooden crates. Some of the older boys were sent to the store site to glean the more useful boards from the crates. These were hauled back to the school and the boys hammered out any nails. The fathers were then called upon to shore up our dilapidated schoolrooms. We had no desks. The few text books were old and musty and obviously begged or borrowed from whom-ever or wherever. The only subjects taught were reading, writing, math, and spelling. Science, history, music, and art were put on the back shelf for lack of books or equipment unless teachers brought along their own supplies. Paper and pen-cils were at a premium, and I found myself writ-ing back to the States for friends to send such items. We heard stories that some schools in the States had shipped such things as out-of-date text books and even old desks. Somehow these never arrived; probably due to pilfering at the ports along the way.

We had a large school ground where the prin-cipal would play baseball with the students. They had no bat, just a wooden stick left over from the crates. Because of the lack of equipment, there were no other sports. One day while playing, one of Robert's shoes disappeared. The students only laughed. I put up such a fuss about it to the embarrassment of my son. There was no way we could buy another pair of shoes his size on the island. It was a back flash to Manado, Indonesia, when the goats had taken one of Bob's shoes and dropped it over a hill in an area where it couldn't be retrieved. Bob wore a size thirteen shoe, and we knew it was useless to drive the many miles to a larger village as the largest Indonesian shoe size was a nine. Many days later Robert's shoe was returned to us as the boys felt sorry for our predicament and retrieved it from where they had hidden it ..... in a trash can.

I started a program to sell hot dogs each Friday noon as a fundraiser. It was a scramble for me to find the wieners or fresh buns for our Friday lunches as the local bakeries often ran out or just decided not to bake that day. Anyway, our luncheons usually came together as parents volunteered to set up tables, and the young students chattered and laughed as they stood behind the tables to serve. One hot dog cost one US dollar, and for this dollar we could purchase one locally made cement block. Our goal was a new school-house. The day came when we could finally call in parent volunteers to construct our new four-room school. The classrooms would be constructed in a row about thirty feet back from the open Pacific Ocean. There would be no extras, just the bare cement-block walls and a blackboard.

By this time, I was volunteering to take over a third-grade class. Luckily, I was assigned to one of our new classrooms. I covered the two long tables with colorful shelf paper. I just loved looking down at all those eager, smiling faces in our lovely, clean schoolroom. I wasn't really a teacher but had taught in similar circumstances in other countries. In reality, teacher shortage or not, I had more experience than a local teacher. Mornings were cheerful until the sun blazed through the windows causing intense heat. Then about two p.m., heavy rains would pelt down and spray through the louvered windows. So on a daily basis, we had to scurry the tables and box seats over to the other side of the room. Within six months, our cement-block walls were a dribble of ugly rust. We were still proud of our labors.

Majuro Co-op School & Arno Island

The older children still had to remain in the original shacks. It was during this time that my son, Robert, broke his arm and was in a full arm cast. There was no functional door in his one-room school shack so the students and teacher routinely climbed in through a window. I was worried about

Robert performing this feat in his unbalanced condition, so I offered to pay to have the door replaced. This turned out to be impossible because the door jams were riddled with termites. We dealt with the situation with much care, helping him through the window and then tying his arm to a beam above for support.

Graduation from the eighth grade came before we left the islands, and what a spectacle that was! Our new building classrooms were decorated with love by the Marshallese. Many had stayed up all night using banana leaves to create a walkway from the door to the make-shift stage. Others had woven huge pandanus mats and placed them on each side of this walkway for the younger students to sit upon. The walls were decorated with huge palm fronds, all adorned with aromatic local flowers. Chairs were set up for relatives, as well as upon the stage for our graduating students - six girls and two boys. I should mention that prior to this event, the mothers had sewn blue floral muumuus for each girl, and the boys had matching blue shirts. I was not allowed to participate in this sewing circle as Karina thought the Marshallese women could do a better job ... oh well!

I suppose there is much more to say about our school system where everyone worked hard, played hard, and created a loving community. A year or so later, when we arrived in California, Robert and Karina were tested to enter the 9th grade and were not behind in any subject. I attribute this to the respect they had for their teachers, and to the fact that they were partially self taught. We had no TV, no newspapers, no libraries or bookstores, and no computers. We relied only on a local radio station. Upon graduation, we had to move on, as the eighth grade was as far as our school went. Children graduating from 12th grade in the Marshallese schools were not reading beyond the third-grade level. So, through a friend, I had them enrolled in a school in Mt. Maunganui, New Zealand. Before making this move, Bob was told that FAO would not renew his contract when it expired at the end of the year as he was past the age of rehire. Wisely, he knew that it would be impossible for him to find a job in New Zealand so suggested we move to Hawaii instead.

The Marshallese live in paradise ..... Please don't disturb them.

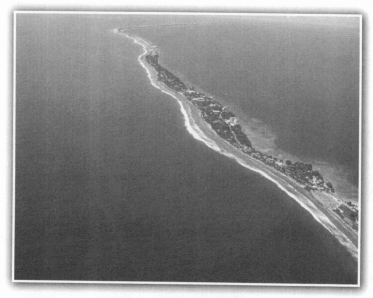

Majuro Atoll

Yokwe Yok! ..... 'til we meet again!

Hawaii

I chose Hilo Hawaii, as there was an extension of the University of Hawaii there. We arrived after a summer's home leave in Canada. Bob joined us to get Robert and Karina settled in school. The first evening there, he told me that he was leaving us and that I should arrange for a divorce. I was devastated, as here we three were sitting in Hilo with no home, family, or job. Why hadn't he mentioned this while we were still in Vancouver? All I had was $10,000 in an account and a return air ticket to Majuro. We tried living in Hawaii for six months but the only job I could find was with temporary services for $100.00 a week. School life was equally hard for Robert, as he had found out that Bob was not returning. Karina kept reminding me that many Hawaiian students went to California to study, and if not, they went there after graduation to find a job. There was no other choice but to change our air tickets and move to California. Otherwise, how we loved our island life.

Aloha!

California and thoughts of Europe

I was once asked if I had culture shock living abroad for so many years. My answer was, "No, but I certainly had it each time I returned to the States."

We moved to Lompoc, California, which was a nice safe place to raise the children. For the next ten years, I worked in the California school system and saw the waste that goes on in the schools. Spending was out of line compared to what I was accustomed to, when all we need is to inspire the kids to want to learn, possibly by taking away much of what is available to them.

At school, Robert was reprimanded for not reading what was required, but his English teacher commented that he always had an interesting and educational book in his back pocket. How could she fail him? He was a bookworm!

I now live in Nipomo, and Robert is nearby in Santa Maria. Eight years ago Karina was offered a transfer through her company and now lives in Paris, France. I visit her each spring, and we take trips around Europe - often to some of my favorite places from my youth. The first year we spent a long weekend in Rome. While there, I was curious and decided to call Umberto, my friend from when I lived in Rome in 1963. I thought he would say that he was married with children and had a good life. I just wanted to say hello and not interfere with his life. How wrong I was. After 42 years, he knew exactly who I was. He had tried to find me in Vancouver but there were too many Enns (my maiden name) in the telephone book. He had never married. I did not see him that weekend, but he asked me to call back each day, which I did. He wasn't able to join us for breakfast at the hotel. I just thought, "Why should he after 42 years of not hearing from me?" Back in California we talked a few times by phone. He always urged me to return to Rome so we could meet again.

Karina was very upset when I told her of my intentions and announced that she would not help me in this endeavor. She said, "I don't care if he is the King of Spain. A lot can happen in 42 years." I still wanted to make the train trip to Rome, but on my next visit to Paris I fainted in the market and landed in the emergency room. My trip was now definitely off. We still spoke by phone, and he often asked why I had not stayed in Rome in 1963 and taken a job with FAO there, a possibility I had never thought of. He never returned to New York, as he had to remain in Rome to take care of his mother, and then later his dad. He had a very successful medical practice but hinted that he did not have a particularly happy life. I inquired if he was well and he answered, "yes," but he also said that he almost never went outside. He added that the streets were too crowded, and he didn't like the people. I assumed from his address that he lived in a nice home not too far from the Colosseum. I finally concluded that he wasn't well and had become an eccentric. We continued to talk on the phone from time to time but I have not heard from him now in a long time. Oh, but how I wish I knew what happened to him.

Since Karina lives in Paris, I now have the opportunity of spending four or five weeks there each spring. This renewed connection to Europe provides me plenty of adventure and many moments of quiet reflection. When I find myself wondering what my life would have been like if I had stayed in Rome so many years ago, I whisper the last lines of Robert Frost's poem, "The Road Not Taken".

> I shall be telling this with a sigh
> Somewhere ages and ages hence:
> Two roads diverged in a wood, and I--
> I took the one less traveled by,
> And that has made all the difference.

ADDENDUM

*B*ob's desire for a divorce was devastating of course; especially considering all we had been through together over seventeen years. My job in Hilo managed to keep my children and me afloat for a short time. This new unexpected chapter in my life scared me; however, as I looked back on the other completely unplanned chapters I had experienced, I realized that they were all part of an exciting, unique mozaic - from the friendly atmosphere of Denmark, to the romance of Italy, to the combination of luxury and bare subsistence, living in Panama and then the simple warmth of the South Pacific. All had enriched me and given the children unbelievable, different experiences they will never forget. Suddenly I knew we'd survive and weave a new and beautiful existence. So in six months we moved to the States, settling in Lompoc, California, where I worked for the school district and my teenagers finished high school.